BARE NAKED

FIEN KESTELYN

BARE
NAKED

The journey of a single woman

For Ella and Lea

I have tried to recreate events, locales and conversations from my memories of them. In some instances I have changed the names of individuals and places to maintain their anonymity. I may have changed some identifying characteristics and details such as physical properties, occupations, and places of residence.

TABLE OF CONTENTS

I abruptly woke up with the most common fear after a night of serious drinking—*where the hell is my phone?*

Next, a sudden realization—*wait a minute, I'm not at home.*

I was in a hotel room.

My brain was in between a state of consciousness and one of intoxication, and my tongue felt like it had been eating sand for the last couple of hours.

The fear went from my phone to its natural habitat—*where is my bag?*

It was nowhere to be found. I could see my coat on the floor, one shoe with a heel and one without scattered across the carpet, my gray silky jumpsuit, and my bra next to the bed.

Where am I?

I had to backtrack—I was at a sales meeting for work in the center of Brussels. We'd been working for days on end. There were presentations until late last night. Without having dinner, I went to a party in an old church converted to a club somewhere downtown. And I drank. A lot.

Suddenly, I looked to the left and saw a man next to me. He was lying on his belly and had a full head of dark curly hair. I was trying to remember what the hell had happened last night; we had drunk cocktails that were basically pure alcohol. I remember snippets of dancing, being in a bathroom, losing a heel, going to a different bar, making out, coming back to the hotel, and seeing some colleagues who were already up to start work the next morning. It felt like a bad dream surrounded by cigarettes, alcohol, and a foul smell.

The man next to me woke up, and I realized it was a colleague. I had always admired the way he did his job, but this all seemed to have gotten a little out of control.

Maybe if I didn't leave the hotel room, I wouldn't have to deal with all of this. Just not today. I wasn't ready to go back to the real world, to my apartment where I lived with my boyfriend, to realizing life as I had known it would now be over.

MY STORY, OUR STORY

After I split up with my boyfriend, I told my mom I wouldn't be single for long. I was confident that within the year, I would be in another long-term relationship. A decade later, my parents haven't met a single boyfriend.

I have been obsessed with being single. Obsessed with *not* being single actually. I felt like being single was a punishment for doing something wrong, and being in a relationship was a reward for doing something right. It made me try really hard to be better, evolve, and grow. I read a ton of books and took many courses trying to figure out what I was doing wrong. Why everyone seemed to have no problem finding partner after partner, and why I was the only one who never got to that part.

In my pursuit of a relationship, I accidentally became a better version of myself. Sometimes gut reigned, sometimes ego, but my actions were always my choice. I changed jobs four times, moved around—from Belgium to Amsterdam and across the Atlantic—traveled the world, and had a life-changing ayahuasca experience. But every time I met a man I liked, I was willing to give it all up and seemed to forget about the path I was destined to take. Lucky for me, the universe never let me settle.

I don't think being single is always fun. It can suck a lot. Some women choose to be single over being in a relationship. While I tried to make myself believe I didn't want a partner, my singledom has never been by choice, but it was also the best thing that ever happened to me.

And I am still single.

In recording this often messy, at times incredibly wonderful, and at other times painfully lonely trek, my aim is to shine light on the experiences that so many women go through.

In the past nine years, I have met many women all around the world and the stories they tell are not so different than mine. Some themes are universal. It seems there's a point in every conversation among women where you can decide to take a turn and start talking about the stuff that really matters. Questions about boyfriends, girlfriends, husbands, children or not wanting or having any, families, break-ups, divorces, sex, menopause— and the vulnerable answers that you get when you're brave enough to ask. In a matter of seconds, that warm feeling of sisterhood appears. Even if you didn't know each other before or will never see each other again, the power of these women and their stories stuck with me.

Our stories connect us to each other. Even though I am most definitely an expert at being single, I am not trying to teach anyone a lesson. I learn the most from hearing stories, and these wonderful women helped me be brave enough to share my own.

BARE-NAKED

In this book, I take off all the layers and put it out there. For you and for everyone.

It's an unpacking of things that you usually don't share with people beyond your inner circle. I love all the beauty in the world, but I think we could benefit from some radical honesty. We could all use some bare-naked, ugly-crying, left-out-in-the-open, up-for-grabs vulnerability. Knowing and feeling each other's joys, sorrows, pains, and pleasures are powerful ways to cultivate greater compassion and connection. We don't need perfection, just openness.

I wrote this book for every woman who is looking for something. Maybe it's a relationship, but it could also be a job, a baby, a calling, a relocation, a big change, or some clarity around yourself—your worth, your needs, your power, your voice. I am not here to say my journey has been a joyride—that's not my experience—but it was the only one for me. If you decide to trust your gut, it will take you beyond what you have ever been able to think up.

Just to be clear, for me, men are not the enemy. I love them very much (and my story attests to it), and nothing in my book is a crusade against them. And just as it is not easy being a woman, it is not easy being a man, either. We as women, often end up confusing them. We want to be strong and independent most days, but we also want to be swept away, held, and treasured on other days. The stories of the men in my life are as much a testimony to their struggles as to mine. I don't approve of all their behavior and certainly didn't deserve being the recipient of some of it, but I can look all of them right in the eyes, maybe with tears, but without any hatred. In fact, each of them helped me to get to know myself better. To shed some light on hidden parts of myself, gain my voice and clarify my vision. For that, I am grateful. I wish them all the best.

In these times, it often doesn't feel comfortable to talk about gender. My experience with finding my softer side has been revolutionary and has opened me up to so much. If at any time the word "feminine" or "masculine" doesn't feel right for you, feel free to replace "feminine" with "yin" and "masculine" with "yang." This book is about people, not about labels.

BELGIUM
THE SEARCH

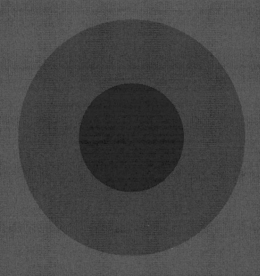

JACOB

I'd met my boyfriend three years earlier. I was twenty two years old, finishing a master's in business communications, and living in a shitty apartment near a small train station in Ghent with two of my best friends. I managed to convince my parents to let me work at a bar owned by one of their acquaintances. Every Thursday night I would earn some extra money at this friendly bowling alley in the middle of the student neighborhood. The nights flew by while I was busy serving drinks behind a large wooden bar to girls wondering what their next move would be, boys who already had too many drinks, or older men who had nowhere else to go.

My mom made the owner promise to send me home by taxi, but usually my apartment wasn't the final destination. Most of the time the car dropped me off at one of the most famous bars in Ghent called The Charlatan. My best friends would already have been there partying for a couple of hours when I'd meet them after work. That night wasn't any different when I made my way through the sweaty masses at 2:00 a.m., looking for my best friend, Charlie.

Charlie and I had been best friends since the beginning of high school, and we were finally living in the same city again. We were making up for lost time, spending countless nights roaming the bars we liked. She was skinny, bubbly, and sometimes painfully straightforward and loved a little drama here and there.

I met Jacob when I was looking for a light, and he happened to be the one nearby. Jacob was a lanky guy with a big head of thick brown hair. He was witty and made me laugh a lot throughout the evening. I walked over to him every time I wanted to light up a cigarette, and by the end of the night, we were lost in conversation. Charlie had to come find me when the bar closed around 6:00 a.m. and the herd of drunk people had to move outside. Jacob walked us back to our apartment where I made him coffee, which was way too strong, but he drank it anyway. We both needed the caffeine. We planned to meet again at the same bar the following Thursday but didn't exchange numbers.

I dragged one of my friends with me the next week and almost gave up on Jacob, until he showed up just after 1:00 a.m.. He convinced me he'd been trying to rally up his friends to join him. My annoyance disappeared after minutes, and we ended up talking and laughing all night until we walked back to his apartment holding hands. I remember the simplicity of the moment, and I imagine it had to do with youth and the fact I liked him so much.

He told me that night he had been walking around the city all week listening to music knowing he had met a great girl he was in love with. There was no doubt in his mind that we were going to be together. I admired his confidence because I had spent the week in agony that he might not like me back. That was usually how I spent the first weeks after meeting someone I liked. On the verge of a panic attack. I could never understand what people actually enjoyed about being in love when I was usually suffering, beating myself up about whether or not they would like me, too. Only when I got a temporary confirmation, was I able to relax and surrender somewhat, but unfortunately, that is not how new found love works.

It took a lot of convincing on Jacob's part to get me to snap out of my anxiety, but he never seemed to feel worried about it. He sent me funny texts, and the best move he made was to send me an email with the YouTube video of the song "Words Don't Come Easy to Me," after we had an awkward phone conversation.

After a couple of months, we were officially boyfriend and girlfriend, and I was sure I had met my match. He was calm, insanely talented and made me laugh every day. I would call him often and his voice always soothed me. Jacob was it for me and it wasn't weird that after less than a year we decided to move in together. A friend of mine from volleyball lived in a wonderful duplex apartment in the middle of the city with a kitchen island and a patio for a price that felt like a steal. In the spring, she called me saying she and her boyfriend were moving out, and my dream apartment was ours. Even though it was early in our relationship, it seemed like all the stars had aligned.

CRACKS

The summer of our first year together, Jacob and I went on a magical trip to Prague and Croatia. Jacob also happened to be an accomplished composer, and even though he had chosen film school for his undergrad major, I always felt he was doing the same thing with images as he had done before with musical notes. He was incredibly talented. At the age of fourteen, he had won the most prestigious contest there was to win for a young composer in the Benelux. His prize was attending classical music concerts anywhere in the world, and as he had never cashed it in, he decided to take me on a musical trip. We spent the days hiking and eating and making love, going to concerts, and savoring every minute we spent together. He took countless pictures of our early intimate moments together with an analogue camera.

I soon found out that with his talent also came a lot of baggage. During a concert in Dubrovnik, he had a meltdown and felt extremely anxious. Somehow this concert had triggered him into feeling that he hadn't been writing enough music and that everything had gone downhill for him in his life since he'd won that contest. We had to leave the venue, and walking home, I helped him the only way I knew how. We talked all night, and he ended up feeling better, out of his head and back in the room on our vacation with me in his arms. It wouldn't be the last time that kind of meltdown happened. Every couple of months I would find myself consoling him and making plans to save his life, motivating him, and going the extra mile to make him feel better. When he did, it felt like an accomplishment. I knew he had lots of potential, the only thing I had to do was to be understanding and show him the way, and everything was going to work out the way I planned.

However, after two years of relationship some situations would come up, and I would lose him. Two days before a wedding we had planned to attend, he wasn't feeling well and didn't want to go. He ended up sitting outside for most of the evening. Sometimes when my friends came for dinner, he'd stay on the other floor of the apartment, barely saying hello. For every film, every project, and every job, I felt like I had to lift his spirits, help him resolve all his problems, and get him out of the recurring dark hole that he found himself in. It was foreign to me to let your emotions determine whether or not you would want to attend a social event. I was always up for anything if it meant seeing friends or meeting new people. Wasn't it my job to make him feel better? Wasn't that what I was supposed to be doing for the love of my life?

Things weren't getting better as time moved along. Jacob got nominated for an experimental film festival in Berlin, so we spent ten days in Kreuzberg. It was the coolest neighborhood in a city full of creatives. In those ten days, I maxed out my lifetime capacity of experimental film watching, but wasn't that what a good girlfriend did? Jacob was very anxious throughout the entire festival and didn't want to talk to the people in charge who had brought him there. I kept on pushing him and resumed my usual role of his personal hype-man.

One night we were arguing in our apartment, and I couldn't understand how he had all these opportunities waiting for him that he wasn't taking advantage of. Suddenly, I realized that nothing was ever going to change and that I couldn't keep doing this. He wasn't growing at the pace I wanted him to and I couldn't keep trying for the both of us.

Coming home from this trip made me see a crack in our foundation that hadn't been there before, and I didn't know if I would ever be able to unsee it. I tried covering it up, because I wanted to go back to the solid belief that we, as a couple, would never crumble, but in the back of my mind, the possibility appeared that it soon could all come crashing down.

THE NEW GUY

That summer, I joined a different volleyball team with some of my friends. It was a very spirited club with teams competing in both the top men's and women's divisions in the country. Volleyball had always felt like home to me. My mother was an amazing volleyball player, and lots of my childhood memories were from the excitement, passion, and joy surrounding this team sport.

From the moment I set foot on the new team's court, it felt familiar. The women's team had been together for a while but immediately accepted us. Most of them were local, and they were used to going out, sharing beers and banter till long after the game had finished.

After every match and practice, we would spend hours in the locker room reviewing what we had just done or chatting about whatever was going on in our lives, drinking sparkling wine, and eating snacks, eventually taking a shower and spending way too long in front of the mirror.

It felt kind of exhilarating walking into the bar where the men's team had been spending at least the last hour drinking and maybe secretly waiting for us.

From the start, a six-foot-five man caught my eye. He had dark hair, broad shoulders, piercing blue eyes, and a strong jawline with a five o'clock shadow. We hadn't met before, but he represented everything I thought Jacob was missing. He was a strong, confident man a woman could lean on; he was ambitious and established and didn't hesitate to go after what he wanted.

On Fridays, we had practice next to the men's team, and I felt like a teenager. I always knew where this guy, Dennis, was on the court. There were looks and faint smiles exchanged and later social media accounts, phone numbers, and texts even though both of us were taken. I honestly didn't expect it ever would turn out to be an issue. I never thought I was going to cross a line. Jacob was it for me, and I figured that after almost three years of being together, I was bound to meet someone that I found interesting, attractive, and different from my partner. So, it was not unexpected and not a big deal. I even told Jacob about the guy, making jokes about it, never thinking it could change anything between us. A couple of months before, I'd had a crush on someone from work, but after a couple of weeks, it faded, and I thought this time it wouldn't be any different.

However, every weekend, I stayed out longer and longer, both Friday and Saturday evenings with the girls, sometimes with the guys too, going out and coming home late.

I was spending all my time working my dream job in fashion, seeing my friends and playing volleyball 3 times a week, pushing my relationship out of my busy schedule. Sunday had always been date night, but even that began to fade. More gaps started to appear in my strong belief about my relationship with Jacob, and I didn't know what to do with them. There were times I couldn't count on my boyfriend, and how was I going to build a future with him if he would be feeling down for a couple of weeks on end? I started saying that maybe I didn't want children, something I'd always thought was a given, but the truth was, I didn't know how I would be able to pull it off in a relationship with Jacob.

BROKEN

There were no secrets between me and Jacob. I shared absolutely everything I was thinking, so when I called him the day after the event where I woke up in the hotel room—I couldn't act like nothing happened. Jacob was as always so nice to me on the phone, calling me sweetie, and all I could say was that something happened with someone else. He first thought that I was making a joke, but when he realized I was serious, there was dead silence, and I could hear something break.

When I got back to our apartment, I found him hinged over on a kitchen chair. He'd gone into a rage after we'd hung up, messed up the work van, and called one of his good friends. He was in limbo, wanting to hear what happened and wishing he'd never asked. I only told him parts of that evening after seeing how every piece of information made him cringe. The conversation wasn't very long, and he asked me to leave the apartment while he was processing everything.

The rest of the weekend I stayed with my close friend Gabrielle and her sister feeling like a piece of shit. Gabrielle and I had known each other since we were twelve. We had been in the regional and national volleyball teams together, and even though we had years where we didn't see each other a lot, we had an undeniable bond. She would never judge and came to pick me up immediately without asking any questions.

Everything reminded me of Jacob and what I'd done and the parts I had not told him yet. All the songs I heard were about cheating or adultery and guilt kicked in big time. Adele's song was the soundtrack for these couple of weeks. All I heard was, "We could have had it a-l-l-l-l-l-l-l-l" and "You had my heart inside of your hand, and you played it to the beat."

I felt like the worst, but somewhere deep inside me, I knew that it would all make sense in the end. I felt awful seeing the person I loved so broken, but something had snapped inside me too. What made me do something I swore I'd never do? Could I go on now after seeing everything clearer than ever, having done what I did, and noticing that there were other men available who I would not feel obligated to take care of all the time. I'd felt something in that hotel room that I'd forgotten I had—a feminine fire I forgot existed.

I tried to give us another chance. The previous three years couldn't all have been for nothing, and I wasn't the one to give up. I knew it was more than just a bump in the road, but I could fix this as always. I couldn't stop myself from talking to Dennis, and even though my brain was going on and on about how wrong this all was, my body had a mind of its own, leaving all rationale behind. After six weeks, Jacob found my phone under my pillow and read the texts which weren't really wrong, but the fact that I was supposed to be mending things instead of texting another man in the middle of the night meant the end for him. We broke up one week before our anniversary and he moved to Brussels.

SAVIOR

After the dust had settled, I realized I didn't have the energy left to keep on doing what I'd been doing in my relationship with Jacob. I had created this role for myself of being the rescuer and had exerted myself with all my planning and checking, saving, and helping Jacob. It was a pattern I not only had created in romantic relationships, but also in friendships. My best friend Charlie had been in an off-and-on relationship for over ten years at that point. I had spent countless hours trying to convince her to have the strength to leave the guy and it had driven a wedge between us many times. But the thing is, she never asked me to save her. She was just telling her story, and I decided I was going to get her out of the situation. I made it my duty to help her. I remember the disappointment that felt like heartbreak when she would go back to him for the millionth time. I felt like I had failed.

Why did I attach my self-worth to helping people? It was a recurrent pattern I started to see, helping, and receiving praise for it. That was exactly what I'd done with Jacob.

When he wasn't sure what he wanted to do, I'd make a plan to get him back on track. I'd been so focused on helping him that I'd completely missed that it hadn't been working, neither for me nor for him.

It was the way my family operated. Opinions and free advice were always readily available. There was always the way you should be doing things. It was a way of showing love, of showing you cared, and protecting the ones you loved from failure, disappointment, and society's disapproval. Unconsciously, I had personally interpreted these remarks as my family telling me, "You are doing something wrong. Please do it the right way," or, "If you don't do it our way, you're not worthy." It also became my way to show I cared about or protected the people I loved. It was so easy for me, making plans and getting things done. The fixing of things was highly valued in my family. Listening, letting people find their way, and simply being supportive were foreign concepts.

In retrospect, I also couldn't fully grasp how personal and intense the creative process was for Jacob. To me it was a job that had to get done, but only later did I realize it was much more than that. He poured his heart and soul out into his work, and his art played by different rules. I wanted him to reach his full potential by making sure he was happy and had his plans straight. I made it my job; I was even changing my dreams to fit in the mold of my making, but after three years and the sobering experience of abandoning my belief system and cheating on him, I had no other choice but to assess the situation. What exactly had gone wrong that led me to blow up my entire life and start over? My body had decided for me; now, my head had to deal with it. Later I would see that the life I thought I wanted wasn't for me. If it hadn't been for what had happened, I likely never would have left Jacob. The universe had other plans for me.

Jacob was my first experience of an adult relationship, and I am eternally grateful for it. I truly loved him. We laughed every day, had inside jokes, and knew each other better than anyone.

It didn't work out with the new guy, Dennis, either. It turned out we needed each other to get out of our relationships, but when that happened, it felt like the spell was broken. I wanted to be with him, but I couldn't find a way to communicate it. We kept seeing each other, met up a couple of times, and a few months later, he moved away. It would only be the first step of my journey as it wasn't my time to settle. The greatness I asked for since I was a child wasn't reflected in the way I'd been living my life. I was just a twenty-four-year-old pretending to be an adult. I thought I had to plan out the next thirty years, but I was only getting started.

SHIELD

I started questioning why I'd picked Jacob as my boy-friend. Why did I hold on for so long?

Since I was an adolescent, I had been constructing a list of characteristics my potential partner had to have, and I applied it to all the guys I met. They had to be tall, smart, creative, driven, educated, successful, and have style before I would consider them as a potential partner. I would analyze whether a person would fit into that perfect image and project it onto a man from the moment we met. This strategy didn't consider my feelings, my heart, or what my body needed and was telling me. I didn't want to leave anything up to chance and thought controlling my destiny was the best thing I could do to not get hurt. It was a nice, thick cozy blanket that I thought was keeping me safe, but instead, I created an armor to protect me from the heartache I didn't want to experience, the pain I unconsciously wanted to shield myself from.

I was convinced that having the right person next to me would make me look better and consequentially make me feel happy. It had given me a false sense of control but hadn't been what I needed. I was making choices on matters of the heart with my head, and nothing good could come from it.

7.
WILD CHILD

The months after Jacob and I broke up, I avoided my apartment that we had once shared like the plague. I couldn't stand to stay in the ruins of my former life because it reminded me of how I was no longer a part of the exclusive club that only had two members. I remember the first day that I went to the apartment alone. I didn't have any plans that evening after work even though I was already a couple of months into singledom. Before, I'd made sure I always had something planned, so I could come home exhausted afterward and crawl into bed. That evening I ended up calling my mother, bawling my eyes out all the way home from work. The anxiety that appeared was all-consuming. All I wanted was something or someone to take me out of this black hole.

Before, smoking had been strictly confined to a social setting, but it quickly became a means of not wanting to feel, or sometimes, not wanting to cook dinner. I was the skinniest I'd been in a long time, and I certainly wasn't a billboard for a healthy lifestyle. When I wasn't playing volleyball, I was working ten hours a day. The weekends began and ended with going out till the sun came up. My friend Charlie and I both had something to run from. She was running from her relationship, and I was running from not having one. We were out almost seven nights a week. Starting with a concert on Mondays or Tuesdays, dinner on Wednesdays, drinks on Thursdays, and long sessions on weekends. Sometimes Sundays were on the table because I didn't want to spend the couples' night alone in my former couples' apartment.

VIDEO

Everything started and ended in the same neighborhood in Ghent. The bar we frequented had blue walls, a colorful but no-nonsense interior, and the closing hour was way past any closing hour in the US. It was called Video, and Charlie and I went there a couple of times a week. It was guaranteed that every time we went there, we were going to see someone I knew. We knew all of the staff, the DJs, the people, and the crowd. It had a great legacy, all artists and musicians and all-round weirdos felt at home there. The place was familiar, exciting and new at the same time. Everyone there seemed to be looking for that same comfort that the place offered, whether they were looking for something or trying to forget. The place had an atmosphere that was unique and peculiar. I felt normal or accepted or however I wanted to feel that night. After 10:00 p.m., the DJ started playing, and we all ended up on the dance floor.

ON THE PROWL

From the moment I was single, the men came flocking. There was something about a distressed young woman who had something to forget or who didn't want to feel that was limitlessly attractive to a lot of guys. I remember being on the prowl everywhere I went. The space got assessed, and potential targets were localized. Everything got registered and evaluated as usual–how tall the guys were, how good-looking, if I knew them, whether they did something creative or cool or not. I was always paying attention. In the moments of darkness at the bar or club, some men seemed to have everything I wanted.

I dressed in black with a big head of curly hair in a short skirt or high heels. Adding that dimension to my six feet seemed to make an impression, or it helped keep people away. Sometimes I lured them over to come and talk to me. Other times a couple of drinks made me take the first step and strike up a conversation. Even if I had fun with my friends, the night didn't seem successful if I hadn't talked to a guy, met someone new or enjoyed any form of romance.

Those conversations would lead to more or the promise of more in the future. It could be texts, dates, sex, a fling, or a relationship. Sometimes, it would last one week, one or several months, or it could start and end all in one night.

A one-night stand for me was pretending, at least for a limited amount of time, that I was indeed part of a team again and receiving affection that I could soak up in every one of my cells. It made me feel like I belonged. The point was to not feel alone. Monday would be ruthless and replace that feeling of unity with isolation and anxiety, both of which I had been trying to avoid all weekend. On Wednesday, the memory would fade and get replaced with permission to do it all over again.

Creative, handsome, and talented guys were the usual suspects. There was a professor, an entrepreneur, a couple of DJs, another filmmaker, a graphic designer, a musician, an artist, and a photographer. It wasn't like I was deliberately picking them out, not exactly, but these traits worked as an aphrodisiac. The bars we frequented were filled with creatives and I was drawn to them. A part of it was status or validation, or the fact that I was impressed by how they had the courage to go down this more dangerous, creative path when I didn't have the guts to try it myself.

A lot of my girlfriends were single and dealing with the same crap. I heard horror stories of what they endured— guys who finished after one minute, guys who sweated like crazy, farted, fell asleep, smelled, snored, or were unbelievably rude and treated them like dirt. And there were more disasters, including getting your period when you didn't expect it, having to go to the pharmacy for the morning-after pill, or being abandoned from the moment the act was done.

My experiences usually didn't feel as dramatic. Alcohol helped me surrender. With the right amount, it was like my brain shut off for once, and my body took over. One friend of mine didn't want to kiss the guys she'd end up with and would kick them out before the night was over, but for me it was the opposite. It also almost always ended up being more than one night because one night was not what I was after.

PUZZLED

Even though I was on the hunt and unsure what I wanted to do with my love life, I considered having relationships with a number of those men, but I was simply unable to express what was going on beneath the surface. Most of the time, the guy involved couldn't see how I felt, and it ended up making them feel extremely confused. When I felt I wanted to start something new, I could never gather the courage to show them how I felt. Or there was so much anxiety and stress that came with those feelings that I tried everything in my power to shove them back down. The only people I would tell the entire story to were my best girls. Charlie could always tell when there was a guy I liked in our vicinity. I would act extremely awkward, be quiet, and nothing that came out of my mouth would make sense. She would whisper, "What's going on with you?" but I usually couldn't snap out of it. Only a drink would make me feel a little less self-conscious.

11.
CLOSE CALL

One boy got close. He was younger than me and a journalist, had glasses, a couple of earrings, and a big mouth. We knew him from Video, and he joined me and my girlfriends for a couple of nights at the bar. While being buzzed at my grandma's Christmas party, I reached out to him on Facebook. I say "reached out," but I just "poked" him when it was still a thing. He made it very publicly clear that it was never a thing. But still, contact was made, and a day later, we were out having drinks. After that day, we started hanging out all the time. What was refreshing about him is he took a lot of initiative. He took me to a Black Keys concert, and different bars and restaurants in the area, and for about two months, we talked daily.

I liked him. He made me feel good, but the critical voice inside me just wouldn't let me have it. I kept on saying how he was younger than me and was too short and didn't have a fancy degree, which was all part of the list of attributes I had made up with my rational mind. After two months, the saboteur had taken over completely and was making me doubt everything about him. My head kept playing the loop of these so-called deal breakers, and when he was away for a week, I didn't text him once. I kept thinking I was probably better off without him and that I should end it. When I saw him after he came back, I was so happy to see him, but I had already blown it. He wasn't going to put his heart on the line again.

Apparently it was too soon for me to give it a chance. I couldn't follow my heart over my brain. I thought I needed to choose with my head first. I never wanted to officially start something with a guy who I didn't think could be the love of my life. Flirtation or flings were ok, but when it came to a real relationship, there was no room for playing. No wonder I was stressed out at the start of any new thing because, for me, I couldn't just see if it fit, it was all very serious.

SUPPORT

During that time my family was worried about me. Yes, I had a job that I put a lot of effort into, but I was also late for family dinners, many times. They saw that my face was plastered with make-up, and they were probably wondering what was beneath it. Youth comes in handy when you're going off three hours of sleep a night. My siblings were all married by that time, and when I broke up with my boyfriend, my dad felt like he had to step in again. He took the role of being the man in my life trying to keep me on what he thought was the right track.

Every phone conversation we had, he would ask me if I had already found a boyfriend or if something was going on. Like I wasn't paying much attention to that part of my life and he had to remind me to put some effort in. It apparently wasn't clear that I was spending all my time focusing on that area. Many things were usually going on, but never anything I would want my dad to know. My mom would know more, but never a lot of details. I would tell her I was going to see a friend in Antwerp, or hang out in Brussels for the weekend.

I struggled for a couple of years with being the only one in my family who wasn't married or didn't own a house, which made me feel like an outcast. I would hide behind humor, making jokes with my godfather telling him I was going to bring my boyfriend *or* girlfriend next time.

To this day I am still the odd one out. I assumed that they were thinking I wasn't good enough, but that wasn't true. They only wanted me to be happy, and after a couple of years, they stopped asking me about boyfriends and settling down. The questions weren't so different for my cousin who had trouble conceiving or my aunt who was battling depression. My family would always support me whether they understood my lifestyle or not.

13.
LES FILLES

In the madness of all of this—the sleepless nights, the alcohol and cigarettes, the boys—I was carried by my girl-friends. During my studies, I'd shared an apartment with my girlfriends Rae and Lily, and a couple of months after I broke up with Jacob, we moved back in together. Charlie was still living with her boyfriend but came over all the time. They were always talking very openly about every-thing that came to mind—boys, girlfriends, people from work, sex, what they smelled or tasted or thought or went through. Nothing was off the table. I remember getting a little bit quiet when the conversations moved to sex. They would be so specific and had no trouble being extremely graphic. There was something so liberating about putting everything out there, sharing your deepest thoughts and asking whatever you wanted to ask in a safe female circle. With a glass of wine, we dissected and shared our lives while having each other's back no matter what. Opinions were shared, and there was only support and no judgment. There were disagreements and drama at times, but we al-ways ended up back together, on the sofa under a blanket.

We all had heartbreaks and new loves and troubles at work or no work, money troubles, or family hiccups. We shared it all like only women can do.

I found this connection not only in our apartment but also outside of it. It was synchronicity how Charlie and I found Liv and Laura again. Ten years before, we'd worked together at an arts festival near my hometown, and we magically found each other again at a friend's party after all four of us broke off our long-term relationships practically at the same time. After that, we hung out all the time. The nights were intense, hilarious, and frantic with so many topics to cover, wine to consume, bars to frequent, and people to talk to. They were the highlight of my week, even though mornings after were rough. I could unapologetically be myself with them, and they would fully accept me. It was like the young girl inside me could finally escape the voice of the always criticizing parent I had internalized and eat and drink as much as she wanted, stay up as late as she pleased, and be as loud as possible. Since then, though we wouldn't always be in the same city, we always were in each other's lives.

It felt like a crazy couple of years, where my best friends and I were searching and experimenting and dabbling in so many things, getting to know ourselves, and getting a lot of things out of our system. There was a lot of instant gratification and indulgence, but we were also hardworking, and most of the time, we kept our responsibilities. Except for the occasional family dinner or the coffee with a friend I missed because I overslept or was hungover in bed. I always knew this time was fleeting and temporary and not part of who I really was. When I stopped being so hard on myself for dropping the ball from time to time, it almost never happened again.

14.
MAX

It started randomly. When Video's closing time came around again, he was still there talking to someone I thought was his friend. It could also have been a random person figuring out their next move. He was very handsome, tall with dark hair, quite a bit older than me, but I didn't think much of it. He came over to talk to me, and we had a short conversation before he asked if I wanted to spend the night at his place. I had been in a bit of a dry spell when it came to guys, and it was a delicate balancing act. I was not looking for random hookups, but my body was yearning for human touch, to be held by strong arms, and there was nothing like having a man's body next to me to make me feel completely safe—at least for a little while. Having that was all I was looking for that evening.

I walked into his building, up the stairs, and into his living room. We sat on his couch for a bit, drinking more wine that we didn't need. Maybe it was my way of convincing myself I had made the right decision. We ended up making out while the sky changed color, the sun was coming up, and the first rays of light were peeping from the horizon.

Not that much happened beyond making out since I had the idea that if I didn't have actual sex, it wouldn't be that big of a deal. It wouldn't count. It would be a blip in history, and I was just making myself feel better the best way I could. When I woke up a couple of hours later, I wanted to leave. I was so quiet, picking up my belongings without making a sound. I was thinking that I just wanted to leave, without saying anything, back to the real world, back to my life. But then, I thought, *This is not how you were raised, Fienie.*

I gave him a little push and said, "Max, I am going to go home."

His bloodshot eyes opened, and he said, like there was no other way, "No, you have to stay," then dragged me back into his bed and hugged me with all he had. We started where we left off for a little bit.

"I am hungry," he said way past noon, going into his tiny kitchen and grabbing everything he had out of his fridge. He had made bouillabaisse the day before and heated up a bowl for me. I looked around the apartment and saw stacks of adult and kids DVDs and heaps of books stacked around his TV. He taught literature, he told me, at a high school, and he had an eleven-year-old daughter who was only around every other week.

We ate breakfast, which was actually brunch or past lunch, and after I finished, I told him a second time that I was going to go home. "My friends are waiting for me to go have coffee," I said.

He stood up from across the table, looked at me, and said, "You are really beautiful," with a little bit of surprise in his voice. He kissed me again and leaned his entire body against mine.

I finally gave up. I forgot about all my self-imposed rules, all the judgment, the way I should be behaving, and how the day should have gone. I had to rely on my gut feeling, which was saying it was safe where I was.

I finally left a couple of hours later, and it was already getting dark again as Monday was getting closer. I was completely buzzing; nothing could wipe the smile off my face. He didn't have my number, and I didn't have his. This was going to be it, and I was completely okay with the situation. What would I do with a guy who was a teacher, had an eleven-year-old, and was more than ten years older than me? I came home to drama with Charlie and Rae, but nothing could bring me down.

Of course, when you decide you are happy with the course of events and don't expect anything more from a man, they come out of the woodwork. Only one day after I left, he found me on social media. To be fair, I had forgotten my umbrella at his apartment, which could have been interpreted as, "Please contact me," but this time, it had not been my intention. I guess the universe had a different scenario in mind. The umbrella pickup was arranged, and after another and another rendezvous, it quickly turned into a regular thing. We saw each other plenty of times, and our hangouts made the darkness of January more bearable.

In my mind, our relationship had no chance of ever working out. I couldn't picture it. I didn't see how he would fit into my future, so the thought of this becoming a thing didn't even cross my mind.

A good friend of mine, Marie, had mutual friends with Max and couldn't believe her eyes. She couldn't believe his eyes because she kept on mentioning how they were the bluest of blues. She also heard he had been seeing this other girl she knew who was gorgeous, but in those first weeks, I didn't care because he and I were never going to be dating. I felt like I shouldn't care anyway, but the thought of him having something as intimate as I thought we had with someone else did give more than a little sting. In those couple of weeks, I had let my guard down because I never realized it had to be up.

Every encounter with him was intense and freeing, and we talked about everything, stayed up for hours, and drank a lot of wine. We were saving each other from loneliness. I didn't have eyes for anyone else anymore, and I started to wonder if I was sure this thing didn't have a pulse after all. We had built something over the past two months, and I was sure he was enjoying it as much as I was. I had grown accustomed to having him around and was looking forward to our nights together. The feelings had crept up on me, and after two months, I had to admit that I was head over heels with this man whom I had thrown all my rules overboard for from the first night we met. Rules like, "You can't have sex with someone on the first date," and, "If you do, it can never turn into more." My definite no had turned into a softer yes without me even noticing.

15.
DISCONNECT

One night, we decided to go to the movies when the new Tarantino came out. It was the late film, and we spent two hours sitting next to each other, but I could not relax at all. For two hours, I was on the verge of a panic attack, and I couldn't tell you anything about the movie because I wasn't paying attention to what was happening on the screen. I had all these questions for him, but I couldn't come up with the courage to ask him anything because I was afraid of the answer I would get. The only thing I could think of was, Will he take my hand? Please just take my hand. He didn't, and I didn't feel a strong connection the entire night. I was not feeling grounded at all. I sat on the back of his bike while we went to his apartment like we had done so many times before.

We talked like we always did, but I still couldn't relax. He picked up on my shift in energy and started talking about relationships and how he wouldn't be starting a new one any time soon. He had been in a second long-term marriage-type relationship for many years that included children from both of their first marriages. He'd put in so much and wasn't willing to do all of that again to his kid. His words caused an implosion inside me. My mind immediately went to, "I understand," and, "We didn't promise each other anything." I felt like it was even silly of me to think he would want more with me because if he did like me, he would have said something already.

When I would go out with a guy I liked, I would be waiting for him to come to me and start that conversation. I would never take any initiative to say what was on my mind; I'd keep him around but never put my cards on the table. When I told this story to a friend, he responded, "I would have started crying if he would have told me that." His reaction took me by surprise. It hadn't even crossed my mind that I was allowed to react that way, and it was exactly what I wanted to do—start to cry and tell him I liked him and he should be with me.

But I didn't. I nodded, didn't say anything about my feelings, and sat there, drinking wine and changing the subject. He must have thought he got off so easy. We saw each other a couple of times after that, but the disconnect and the loneliness I felt after I had spent the night with him didn't add up. I figured he never stopped seeing other women, and the thought made me sick to my stomach. It all wasn't worth it. Not for someone who was never going to choose me.

I had one relapse during the summer. When I saw him at Video after, he asked me, "What happened? We had so much fun, and you just disappeared."

I finally had the guts to say, "I wanted more than that."

He went quiet and didn't say anything back. I excused myself and left, knowing nothing was going to change, but at least I stood up for what I wanted, which made all the difference in the world to me.

16.
IN NEED OF SCHOOLING

I came to the realization I couldn't do it by myself. I had come to the same point where I had been for what felt like the millionth time. Where, in my eyes, I had given so much, and I still ended up feeling abandoned. And single. Always still single. When was this ever going to change? I created the same loop for myself and couldn't get out.

For the first time, I heard a strong voice inside myself saying, "Reach out, get help." It was not desperation. It felt very clear and calm. I had reached my limit.

Marie had been going to a women's network led by a charismatic therapist. The groups were small, and it had had a tremendous impact on her life. The year before when we had lost one of our dearest friends, Marie had turned to this women's group for support. The group was called The School for Relationships, and it was built for women. Relationships are the focus of the human species. We are here to connect, but that is also the source of most of our grief.

"Spend your money on something else," I'd suggested to Marie exactly twelve months before. "Use that money to go on a trip."

When I started thinking that the women's network was exactly what I needed, I attended one of the introductions to the therapist's work. It was the end of February, still dark and gloomy outside, and people were looking for a sign that spring was finally here. The room was filled with around 50 women of all ages and backgrounds and a handful of men there to support their women. Patricia was a small woman of Dutch-Indonesian descent with shiny black hair that touched her shoulders. She looked perfectly styled and had long, elegant, manicured fingernails with red nail polish. She asked if any of the women in the room had felt depleted in any way. If anyone felt like she had lost her way in relationships and didn't like the role she was in. I nodded my head along with a bunch of women who didn't seem to love where they were finding themselves either.

Patricia explained the principles of feminine and masculine energy and what traits had been attached to each. Feminine energy is patient, receiving, empathetic, sensitive, humble, and caring. Masculine energy is fast, competitive, assertive, goal-oriented, and independent. In every person, there is a balance. Depending on what your core energy is, you need to spend slightly more time in your feminine or masculine energy to recharge your battery.

So many women felt like they had to do both and lost their way to the feminine, forgetting what their core energy was. Too much yang, never enough yin. I sat there, and my jaw dropped. For as long as I could remember, I pushed and conquered, did my best, tried not to complain, went and did even more. When I couldn't use my habit of controlling a situation, I felt completely lost, like a small, wounded child not knowing what to do. There was no resting in my life. I couldn't sit still, or I didn't feel I could. The only place I felt supported and relaxed was with my girlfriends or with a boyfriend, but that hadn't been working out for me lately.

Patricia went on about the connection between the brain, the heart, and the womb, and that connection would be the way to self-love. It also struck a chord with me; for as long as I could remember, I was trying to use my head and ignore the signals my body was giving me. Signals of being tired, signals that volleyball wasn't working for my ankles, back, or neck, or signals I had to stay home from work because I was sick. Nothing a painkiller couldn't fix. The idea I needed to listen to what I needed instead of overruling it with my head came as quite a shock. By the end of the night, I was signed up for the first training starting two weeks later. In two weeks, I would start this journey on Monday evenings with a group of women diving into the depths of my mind.

17.
MONDAYS

I convinced my friend Lucie to go with me, and when I picked her up, I remembered us saying, "We'll be fixed by summer" and "We better be in relationships by that time." Yes, a relationship. It didn't even have to be a good one, any would do.

There were twelve women that first Monday, and by the end of the first half-hour, Lucie was in front of the group bawling her eyes out. Every one of these women had such a strong reason for being there, ranging from, "I am cheating on my husband," to, "My husband cheated on me," "I have never been in a relationship," "I am in a relationship with a married man" or "a younger man." By the end of the first evening, I was overwhelmed with compassion for the stories of every one of these women. I was lost for words and felt such a strong sense of sisterhood with all these ladies I didn't even know before that night. Over the course of eight weeks, we discovered what we were looking for in a relationship and why we were attracted to a specific person, and what it said about us.

REFLECTION

Patricia also taught us that everything that struck a chord with us, whichever emotion came up, could tell us something about ourselves; every coworker, family member, teacher, roommate, or landlord who caused a laugh or a tear told a story about ourselves. A story about old beliefs or wounds controlling our daily experiences. Most people live their lives never looking at these emotions, wondering why the same feelings or patterns keep popping up repeatedly.

Every day, I dug into everything that was triggering me. I always had a notebook with me, so I could write down and dissect every single trigger, so I could take away the power they had over me. "I feel disrespected," "I feel abandoned," and, "I don't feel seen or taken seriously," were only some of the things I was apparently feeling many times every single day. By taking responsibility and being aware of these old beliefs, I began to feel better. But it felt like I was just scratching the surface of what lay buried in my subconsciousness.

When my colleague Poppy and I got into a disagreement, she said, "I made it into your notebook today, didn't I?" You could say I developed a little bit of an obsession. I couldn't stop talking about how wonderful I thought Patricia's school was and how much insight it had given me. I spent hours talking about what I had learned and telling my sister and my friends about every technique, exercise, and conversation, trying to persuade my family and friends this was the way. I couldn't understand why people weren't putting in any effort when consolation was so close. Didn't they want to be happier?

It ended up having a reverse effect. My mother was very concerned and thought things were going the wrong way for me. None of my girlfriends understood why I was sharing my secrets with women I didn't know.

However, my gut was telling me nothing about this was wrong. I had found a softness I somewhere already knew I had. It was so liberating to be amongst women who supported me, who didn't know anything about me and wouldn't judge any of my stories. They were genuinely interested in what I had to say. I could let my tears flow and be carried as long as I needed. I was peeling off the layers and digging deep into the patterns I had been repeating the last decade or probably longer than that. After eight weeks I knew I was not going to be fixed before summer, and it was only just the beginning.

BOUNDARIES

After the first course, I enrolled in the second training. The first exercise set the tone. Often, Patricia would use role-play or physical exercises to let us come to an insight into where we were in the process of healing. We were divided into pairs and were facing each other at about 30 feet apart. The task was simple. "The first part of the exercise one person will slowly cross the space between you two, and when you feel them entering your physical space, you will let them know, and they have to stop." I had never seen boundaries as something physical you could pinpoint in a room. I could feel when someone was getting too close and making me feel uncomfortable, but I had never used that knowledge in different situations. It was weird how I could physically feel the boundary and how far it was from my physical body. As an extravert who thrived on hugs and physical touch, I didn't think I had that many boundaries.

The second part of the exercise was a level up. "This time, even when you tell the person to stop because they've reached your boundary, they will continue walking towards you until they feel you are serious about guarding it. They will not stop approaching you until you make them." This was something else. She told us when you set your boundaries, there is no need to yell or use any sort of violence to defend them. If you are dead serious in the aim to protect them and you express it with gravity, nobody will ever cross that line.

It was my friend Nina who was standing in front of me, and she raised her eyebrows when she heard the assignment. She would be the one approaching me. After only a couple of steps, I felt she'd met my barrier even though she was still twenty feet away. With everything I had, I tried to make Nina stop, but nothing that came out of my mouth was powerful enough. A shrieking, unsure, and silent attempt of a scream wasn't going to keep her back. Every step she took felt like a violation, but there was nothing I could do to make it stop. Nina looked puzzled at Patricia. When I broke down crying, the exercise was over.

A couple of women came and hugged me, but I was inconsolable. Had I let people cross my limit without saying a word? Undoubtedly. Did I not have the power to form a courageous and absolute *no* that made nobody cross my line? I absolutely did not. Most of the time I didn't even feel it because I was living in my head, and it was something that I wasn't supposed to be feeling, but my body was registering everything. I was supposed to be a nice girl who wasn't in the position to say no very often. My life had been filled with family, friends, work, and activities like the lives of my parents had been and the lives of their parents too.

I saw people getting on each other's nerves daily and stepping over personal boundaries without anyone addressing it. It was just the way it was.

All this soul-searching was just the tip of the iceberg, and I was hooked. While my journey of self-development had started with the aim of finding a man, it had shown me so much more. Discovering what had been holding me back, not only in relationships, but also in my entire life, had turned into such a big part of me, where the previous year I hadn't even known it existed.

STUNNED

The years after I broke up with Jacob, my job was my anchor. It was the thing I cared about the most and a reminder of who I was. I was part of the product management team at a denim company working on the women's line, and I felt like it was the best job in the world. There was something about creating a product that was perfect for our consumers that brought me into a state of flow. Getting into her mindset and predicting what she would want in over a year. I couldn't believe how lucky I was.

I started at the bottom, and even though I knew so many girls would kill for the job I had, I was impatient to get to the next step. I had been in a junior-level job for three years, and I was feeling restless. I was dying for a promotion, and I felt ready for one. I dreamed of my boss's position. Managing the women's line, not having to do boring system stuff but defining the strategy and having the final call was all I wanted.

My final evaluation was successful, but when my manager said there was, in the short term, no promotion in the books for me, I started crying. I was inconsolable and didn't know how to proceed. I was yearning for the recognition that I was doing a good job, but it never came in the form I wanted.

After I got back from an amazing trip to the Greek Islands with Lucie—where we talked, ate delicious food, and read books in the sun for eight days straight—I came into the office finding my boss waiting, antsy for me by the vending machine in the lobby. I had never seen her this skittish. She asked how my trip had been but was too distracted to listen to my answer. I followed her up the stairs, and she told me, "Let's go to the third floor," where we usually never had any business being. She opened the door to a white sterile meeting room, and when I saw the lady from HR sitting at the table with a facial expression that reflected a mix of dread, fear, and seriousness, I knew what was about to go down.

My manager explained that there were no career opportunities for me at the company, and they had to let me go. They gave me a generous package with six months' severance and even said they would keep it confidential if I decided I wanted to tell everyone I had left on my terms. I immediately went into survival mode, and I only wanted to get out of the building. Thinking of facing all my colleagues, answering the same questions, made my head spin, and I had to get out of there. I grabbed my phone and started making calls; the first one was to my parents. I tried to not have them freak out as I explained the situation. My friends who worked on the campus came to get me. It felt like it was a dream, and it would take me a while to realize it had happened in real life.

I didn't give myself any time to process. The next day, I made plans to take a job at a festival, which was going on in my hometown of Ghent, for ten days straight. I was trying not to feel the immense sadness of the little girl inside. I had given everything I had to the company, and they hadn't made any investment or space to accommodate my future career. I had worked long hours, learning skills that were not my forte just to show my management how committed I was. I was also blaming myself for my tumultuous private life, which might have influenced my performance over the years, but I felt like the past year I'd been on such a good run. The company letting me go had touched a deep wound —a place inside me that told me I wasn't good enough so I felt I had to give above and beyond to cover it up. I wanted recognition from my managers, and without it, I was lost.

RELEASED

Despite how sad the situation made me feel, I could see the positive of it. Something inside me knew that it could end up being the best thing that happened to me. I was twenty-seven, it was the beginning of summer, and I had six months' pay coming my way which was plenty of time to think about my next move. July was all about working at the festival, having fun, and not looking ahead.

I decided to do something epic with the time I had off. A solo back-packing trip seemed like a no-brainer. I decided to spend a month alone traveling around Thailand. Going by myself was scary and highly uncomfortable, but at least Southeast Asia seemed like a safe bet. I might have been one big millennial cliché, but I didn't care.

From the moment I decided to go on the trip, it seemed like the stars aligned. Tickets were cheap, my friend Chloe's brother Jon was on my flight, and suddenly, everyone had friends in Thailand or people they knew who were there on holiday. If I wasn't careful, nothing was going to be solo about this trip. Chloe and her mother brought us to the airport. We flew on a Middle Eastern airline, and it was the nicest airplane I had ever been on. There were only a handful of people on the plane, and Jon and I were each taking up an entire row of seats. He was flying to Hong Kong to start a new life. He took a job at a big consultancy firm, and he and his girlfriend decided to give this new life a try. We spent the next six hours talking about what had brought us to this point in our lives. It was rare to realize so clearly at the moment that we were both about to embark on what would turn out to be life-changing adventures. I felt strengthened as I said goodbye to Jon and hopeful for what the next month would bring.

Arriving in Bangkok was a culture shock. There were so many intense smells that were new to me and always people surrounding me. I was happy that I stuck out of the crowd by at least a foot. After a couple of days in Bangkok, I took a night train north to Chang Mai. After spending ten hours in a tiny carriage with a middle-aged French couple, I arrived in the far north of this fascinating country. I toured all the temples and went to the Golden Triangle where the Mekong River connected Laos, Myanmar, and Thailand.

I didn't feel alone for one second. It was such a transformative feeling, like I didn't have to be dependent on anyone but myself and everything was working out, like I was being supported. I walked around free from any physical and emotional hurt, not preoccupied with boys, friends, family, or anything, just doing my own thing. I didn't have to take care of anyone, think about how anyone was feeling, and the only question that concerned me was, Where do I want to go next? There was never a plan; I followed my heart and intuition.

In Chang Mai, I took a break from crappy hostels, and I stayed at a nice hotel instead. I was spending my afternoon by the pool and called my sister to tell her about everything I had experienced. My sister was the eldest of the three kids in my family and had always been the perfect child. She was a good student, stayed close to home, and took the path that my parents would have wanted for my brother and me. She had three wonderful children and a smart husband who was also from our hometown and she didn't think there was anything wrong with being in your comfort zone. Even though our lives were vastly different, my siblings had always felt like home to me.

We were having a deep conversation where I was questioning whether my parents were really supportive and how I felt they didn't understand what I was trying to do, going to the other end of the world by myself. My sister interrupted me all of a sudden, saying, "When are you going to realize it's not because you make different choices, we think anything less of you? Because, for us, you are perfect the way you are." I broke down in tears when she spoke those words. At that pivotal moment by the pool in the north of Thailand it clicked, and I could really feel the love my family felt for me.

22.
ALL PLAY

My next destination was Pai, a little hippie town three hours from Chiang Mai. Driving there was representative of how the next couple of days were going to go. I was in the back of a small van with six other young backpackers trying not to get sick while the driver was maneuvering the small, rocky roads that zigzagged along the mountains. I ended up following two girls who already had booked a hostel, which turned out to be quite the party place. The next couple of days I spent drinking lots of beer and driving around on a little moped. I wasn't used to driving on the left side of the road, and all I could think was left, left, left, left, left, left, left.

One of the first people I met at the hostel was a Scottish guy named Jack. He was gorgeous and tall, and the entire first day, I didn't understand half of what he was saying. I remember nodding and thinking, You can say whatever you want. By the second night, I could understand most of the conversation, and by the campfire, he shared a story that made both of us cry. We spent the entire night talking, drinking, and laughing, and I loved it when one of the girls said, "I thought you guys had been together for years." We ended up staying in the same dorm, and I heard him move next to where my friend and I were sleeping, or in my case pretending to sleep. I wondered if he had lost his nerve while he was trying to move close to us. I truly wanted to believe he was moving closer to me, and we would end up spending the rest of our trip traveling together, but none of that happened. He was going to go to Myanmar for the next couple of weeks learning an obscure martial art at a training camp he had booked. Maybe he was interested in me and maybe not. We exchanged some messages, mostly initiated by me, and I finally worked up the nerve to tell him that I regretted not kissing him alongside that campfire. He told me to be more spontaneous, and it was the last I heard of him.

I always had found a way to make romance the focal point. Like the trip would have been better if there was a romance. I am sure we shared a moment, but that was it, just a moment. It made me realize I didn't need a guy to make my trip a success; I could be happy without it.

Halfway into the trip, I moved south. I left all the people I met behind and went off the beaten path to an island called Ko Chang. I had no reason to go there, and I didn't know I wanted to try a diving course, but when I saw a sign, I knew I did. My trip was so different from my daily life where I would contemplate every move, consult friends, and obsessively wonder what the best solution was. Here, I wasn't thinking at all; I was just being.

My final week I wanted to spend on the beach before I went back to the dreary Belgian weather. I spent my days reading, taking yoga classes, and soaking up the sun. The evenings consisted of hours of interesting conversation with three single ladies I met there who were a bit older than me, all of us sharing stories about our past and about our dreams. We were all at a crossroads in our lives, and even though there was an age gap, I felt a strong sisterhood listening to their stories in this tropical place.

One evening we went to the pier downtown to have dinner by the water, and during our second bottle of wine, one of them looked at me and said, "You do know you are surrounded by women who will not have children." I couldn't tell if that was what they all wanted, but it was a fact, and they had accepted the situation. Up to this point, my life had been what I thought it had to be. These ladies seemed to have embraced their lives and their choices, and I could only feel love. They were single and lived exciting lives, they had found their passions and made careers around it. It was the first time I saw adult women who didn't need a relationship to feel complete and didn't obsess about it.

During one of my last days on the island, I was checking my email, and a recruiter had reached out about a job for a leading international sneaker brand that seemed to be everything I had been looking for. During my trip, I hadn't sent one email or applied to any new jobs. I'd decided to let everything go, not think about the future, and deal with reality when I came back. Amid relaxation and surrounded by nature and great company, the perfect job presented itself.

And I got it. I would be moving to Amsterdam. It felt like the universe had spoken, and I was beginning a new chapter in my life.

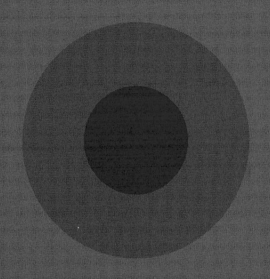

AMSTERDAM
TRANSFORMATION

23.
NEW LIFE

Moving has never been my favorite thing. I always put everything off to the last moment, I had too much stuff and needed the help of my family and friends. My move to Amsterdam was an entirely different experience. It was the first time I really felt the perks of corporate life. Having a moving company was part of the deal and I just watched them pack up all my stuff and drive it to Amsterdam. Temporary housing was also provided, so I had a place to stay until I found an apartment.

When I arrived in Amsterdam, a consultant was there to give me all of the forms, buy me a drink, and welcome me to the city. I was staying at the Grand Krasnapolski, a legendary hotel in the middle of Dam Square, the most central and touristy location in the city. The hotel had been around since the nineteenth century and had an atmosphere of old grandeur. I arrived on Dutch Veterans Day after a parade, and at that time, I was totally oblivious to the lofty status of the establishment where I was staying at. I rolled up into the lobby area wearing sweatpants. The clerk at reception looked at me funny but asked politely, "Checking in?"

After he pulled up my reservation, he immediately picked up the phone and informed someone, "The VIP has arrived." While I always enjoyed it when a friend would put me on the list at a club or party, this took VIP to a whole new level. I was surprised about this new life my job had provided for me, and I hadn't even done anything to deserve it yet. I had never stayed at fancy hotels while growing up and always thought, somewhere deep down, that it was wrong for me to want it. Even though my room was at the back of the hotel overlooking the canals of the red-light district and I woke up to the distinct smell of cannabis, it felt great. I didn't know at the time that asking for a different room was an option.

24.
FAMILIAR FEELING

What gave me the strength to move to Amsterdam besides the job was the fact that Annabelle had moved there a year before. She'd been my friend from the first month of my first job. We had very similar backgrounds, did the same studies, came from the same region in Belgium, and followed similar paths. She would say I followed her path, but that was the price of being two years younger than her. It made me more confident because I knew I could always spend the evening on her couch, drinking wine and watching a romantic comedy that made your toes curl. She felt like home and spoke my language, which made it easier when I had to decide about the job and the move.

MY HOUSE

When I told people that I was moving to Amsterdam, I always got the same reaction: "Wow, Amsterdam! Amazing, but it's so expensive, and the apartments are so small." Apart from feeling annoyed, something inside me always thought, *That won't be my reality.* I simply didn't believe there weren't any spacious and reasonably priced apartments available. I knew one of them would be mine. I started to reach out to every person I knew in Amsterdam or who knew someone in the city, and the day I arrived, I already had two appointments lined up. After my first day on the job, I drove back into the city for my first look at a prospective apartment. It was an amazing historic brick building, more than one-hundred years old, that had been a children's hospital and a school for nurses. It had a courtyard with a garden that all the apartments overlooked. It was a little rundown, but the rooms were huge and had fifteen-foot ceilings. The apartments I looked at were made up of four rooms that were 300 square feet each and had a mezzanine as the bedroom.

As I was visiting the place after my first day of work, I felt overwhelmed by overall newness—new information, new impressions, and new faces—so when I arrived at the front door of the apartment, I was ready for a glass of wine. Unfortunately, they were only offering me a cup of tea. All the housemates were there, and I got a good gauge of the energy in the place.

Thomas was a slender blond guy in his mid-twenties who was a photographer and was writing articles for a newspaper. Paul owned his own record label, was a DJ, and owned a store full of exotic vintage vinyl. We had a great conversation, and I asked a lot of questions, I answered all theirs as well. We looked at the room which was huge and perfect, and the price was reasonable. I couldn't believe my luck. I was surprised and impressed that I had found the apartment I was looking for in an up-and-coming neighborhood on the second day after I arrived.

"I'll take it," I told them, just generally feeling in a great mood. I got a strange stare from the guys and there was an awkward silence. "Uhm, we are actually still seeing five people tonight," they told me.

The only thing I could say was, "Oh, I see." I had no idea.

Luckily, I had won them over with my Belgian charm and probably my ignorance since I didn't know I was competing with a quarter of the twenty-year-olds in the city. The next morning Paul called me and welcomed me into my new home.

After a month, I had to partake in the same interviewing process because we were looking for a new roommate. Iris made the cut. She was a French twiggy, black-haired musician who was also an artist and had been a cage dancer in a former life. She brought a bottle of wine, and after some disappointing candidates, we had a great night, and she was unanimously chosen to be our number one. When Iris moved in, things got even better. We spent our time in the evenings hanging out in the kitchen, sharing food, and talking for hours over wine or tea. We had a lot of visitors hanging out in our apartment, and they all seemed to be doing something creative. All of us loved meeting new people and getting inspired, so one night we came up with the idea to organize monthly soirées.

We had a couple of rules: 1.No phones in the room, 2. Every roommate must invite two people, and 3. No asking the question, "What do you do?" We called it the monthly salon like we were living in Paris in the 1700's. No wonder those nights turned out to be memorable, to say the least. We had amazing, connected conversations, friends passed out, parents were doing shots, there were screaming matches, and some of us found love even if it was only for the night. There was something about that old house with such a rich past paired with a colorful array of people that allowed for an unexpected but wonderful turn of events.

KILLING TIME

Despite all the fun and bubbly atmosphere in the house, this move meant a big change. For the first time in my life, not every hour of every day was jammed full of work, friends, and sports. When I was home, there was extra down-time that I had to fill, and when the roomies were busy, it was hard to adjust. I had never had so much time on my hands or a couple of hours on a weekend with nothing to do. It was such a new sensation to have to divide up my time and not just follow the stream of activities, as I had been doing my entire life. In came a strange feeling of anxiety I hadn't experienced before in that context. The vast amount of time came as a relief at first, but after a couple of months when seasons changed, it transformed, and I was desperately trying to fill not only the spare time but also the emptiness inside.

One of the perks of the job was a gym on site that also offered classes at all hours of the day. I chose to dive into yoga. After twenty years of volleyball, I no longer wanted to be yelled at from the sidelines and explore my internal motivation. I chose the more cardio type of yoga to ease into it. The classes made me feel like I had a proper workout. The hour I was doing it, I wasn't thinking about anything apart from, *I need to get my foot in that direction,* or, *Can I get my arms to do this?.* There was no worrying about the mistake I made ten minutes ago or the service I missed at the beginning of the game or the disappointment I must have been to my coach or teammates or mother. It was free of competition, and I loved it. And it helped me a lot with my anxiety during the day. It sneakily opened the door to other spiritual practices such as meditation and yin yoga. I heard about an app called Headspace that explained meditation as detailed and matter of fact as possible, and I was hooked. It started with ten minutes a day and after a couple of months, I was up to twenty minutes first thing in the morning. My parents and friends would have described me as disorganized and chaotic, but with daily exercise and meditation, it got easier to organize work, start an assignment after finishing another and stop running so late for everything. For the first time in my life, I found my footing.

27.
DIFFERENT TYPE OF CLUB

With the peace of mind I found, I had to admit I did miss volleyball more than expected and especially the game. No aspect of my life came close to the drama, excitement, and emotion of the match. It had regulated my energy and kept me on the straight path without me even recognizing it. With all that time on my hands, I knew that I should throw myself into something that I knew and made me feel better.

I couldn't have chosen a better club. I started late in the season and I had warned the coach I wouldn't be able to attend all the practices because of work and travel, but because of the injury of one of the core players, I was on the court every single week. It was freeing playing because it was for fun and free from all the expectations of earlier performances. Nobody knew anything about me in that sense, and I had never played better. I also found an amazing group of women who felt like sisters. Bonding happened on and off the court, and those girls helped me settle in the city, my new life, and made me feel like family.

28.
MY SECOND JOB

Dating hadn't been going well since I'd left Belgium. You would think in the land where the average man is above six feet, I would be in dating heaven, but I hadn't met anyone I was truly interested in. I had met a friend of Iris and another who was a volleyball player, but both ended up feeling awkward and I had no romantic feelings for them. For a couple of months, I thought I had feelings for a friend from Belgium but after a disastrous trip to New York, we never texted again.

I started dabbling in the world of dating apps to pass the time. It was easy for me in a new city since the apps wouldn't be filled with people I had known for years. The app I was on was called Happn, and it gave you an overview of people you passed during the day. My roommate thought it was hilarious. She imagined she could scan every hot guy she passed on the street with the app and see if he was on it, but unfortunately it didn't work that way.

I went on a handful of dates, one with a guy whose profile looked very promising. He was tall, interesting and a couple of years younger than me. When I saw him, I almost didn't recognize him. He had found the perfect angle to take his pictures, an angle that I, unfortunately, couldn't find in real life. Looks aren't a priority, but I do appreciate a correlation between the online persona and the guy in front of me. He was a bit awkward, gamed a lot, and it was hard work to keep the conversation going.

Dating for me was very serious. I had been single for about three years by then, and I felt like something had to happen soon. I had processed the move, loved my job, and was ready for the next step which for me was a relationship. At this point, dating was not chill or non-committal. I had a goal in mind—being in a serious relationship—and I wasn't going to let anyone take my mind off it. I wasn't sure how I would reach my objective, but I treated it like a job. As always, it was in the back of my mind everywhere I went.

THE CHEF

Suddenly some guy sent me a short message through the app, and I was on the fence about whether I would reply or not. His pictures weren't clear, and his profile didn't say how tall he was, which always made it a bit awkward if I didn't dare to ask ahead. I thought I should wing it when he asked me out, and I agreed to go for a drink at a bar only a couple of blocks from my house. It was a sunny evening in early April. Spring had begun, and I was wearing black jeans, a black shirt, and an oversized royal blue trench coat. I wore a full face of makeup, which always felt like putting on warpaint. I used makeup to feel ready for the evening and to put on a disguise and not immediately show my true colors. I walked into the overcrowded bar a couple of minutes late, and it was full of the usual cool crowd you could find in that part of town. It only took me a couple of seconds to spot the six-foot-seven man by the bar with a man-bun and a tan face. From the first moment I laid eyes on him an infinite amount of information got exchanged, and my decision was made. His pictures didn't do him justice at all.

I made up my mind in that first split second; he was good enough for me.

He ordered us drinks, and we walked outside on the patio and sat down at one of the wooden picnic tables. I felt like a million bucks having drinks with this gorgeous man. He seemed very sweet, a true gentleman, and passionate about what he did. He was a chef and had worked at several restaurants in the city. He was obsessed with his line of work and had been doing it for over a decade. I felt mesmerized, and every time we didn't know what to say, we would smile at each other like teenagers, take a sip, or light up a cigarette. A couple of people he knew came over to say hey to him, and I loved that they thought we were going out. Even though it was a weeknight, the date lasted past my bedtime, and he biked me home through the park as a true Amsterdammer would do.

When we got to my place, I hugged him and went inside before he could think about making a move. I was so happy with how the date went that I didn't want to complicate things. It was stressful deciding what I wanted to happen at the end of a date, but this time, my rules were upheld, and that made me pleased with myself. These rules in my head came from not having any after I broke up with Jacob and it didn't work out well for me. What I learned at The School of Relationships was still ingrained in my mind and made me realize what it was like to feel where my boundaries were; I realized I needed more time than I usually allowed myself to get to know someone new. It felt like every time I met someone I liked, I would give up everything I learned about my personal space and let myself be washed away by the promise of a true connection. I wanted to wait to have sex until I felt it.

Our second date was on a Sunday afternoon. We met for a bike ride in a huge park only a couple of minutes away. He had always lived around my neighborhood, and even though he was in between houses, it was where he was looking for his new home. We stopped at a little café next to a pond where he knew the owner. We talked and laughed while we were drinking tea. Well, at least I was drinking tea; he was drinking beer and having jenever, a local liqueur the Netherlands is famous for. After a couple of hours we biked back to my appartement, and this time, he wasn't going to let me go without a kiss. At our departure point, he jumped off his bike, took my face in his hands, and kissed me for the first time. When I walked up the stairs, I felt like I was walking on clouds.

We texted back and forth but didn't plan any other date until King's Day. Once a year, Amsterdam turned into a big orange blob with festivals and parties on every square and street corner to celebrate the birth of King Willem-Alexander. The country celebrates the king's birthday, and everyone goes all out. Years before, I started going to the celebrations with Annabelle, and we would have an entirely different experience every year. Either we'd walk around the city looking for a hidden treasure at the endless flea markets, visit one of the music festivals outside of the city or we would go the day before to enjoy the celebrations by night. That King's Day, I had celebrated the night before with my roomies and spent the day on Annabelle's couch drinking wine in Amsterdam Noord where she'd lived with her boyfriend. The chef hadn't had that day off in years and spent the entire day cooking for his friends and drinking while looking out the window of his friend's apartment overlooking the canals. During the day, we texted back and forth, and at the day's end, he wanted to meet up.

A nagging feeling deep inside my stomach told me that it wasn't a good idea; it would be better if we met up some other day after sleeping off all the alcohol we had consumed. But this was the guy I had been daydreaming about all week, and both my ego and my inner child couldn't wait to see him again. I couldn't believe he liked me, and I didn't want to do anything to mess it up or put him off. From the moment we met up, I could see his eyes were blurry and small, and he had more than enough to drink. I opened the door to my apartment, and when he kissed me, he made a sound of relief, which triggered me. I started thinking that this wasn't a good idea at all. We went into my room and started making out on the sofa. My entire body was buzzing because all I wanted was to kiss him, but he had bigger plans for the evening. I had realized over the years that sex clouded my judgment. Having sex with a guy I liked made me attached much more quickly and made me lose my anchor. I didn't know what the best timing was, but I wanted to hold off longer than I had in the past to make sure I was 100% into it.

The making out intensified. He was following his hands all over and under me. I was still enjoying it, but something inside told me tonight was not the night to have sex, and I would rather wait till we were both sober to move forward.

I had only seen him three times, and it just didn't feel right. He was trying to take my top off, and I looked at him and said, "Not much is going to happen tonight."

The look on his face was like a young child who had just been punished. His sad and vulnerable facial expression had a hint of shame and made me feel so bad that I had caused this reaction. I kissed him to try to make him feel better, and we resumed where we left off. When we reached my limit again, I said, "No, let's not."

He seemed confused but stopped what he was doing. My body was begging me to be strong and make it end, but at the same time, my head was arguing, "What's the problem? You like this guy so much, and he is interested, so just get on with it."

The third time I said no, it wasn't strong anymore. I was questioning if it wasn't what I wanted because parts of my body were enjoying what we were doing. I wasn't sure, and he didn't take me seriously.

I was reminded of the exercise about boundaries during the women's group. I felt his actions had surpassed mine, but I didn't dare to push back and stand up for what was right for me.

We ended up going to my bedroom, it was sort of a symbolic move too. I'd left myself behind in the sitting room as my body moved to the bedroom. I gave away my power to make the guy I liked, like me back.

Even still, the sex we had was overwhelming. Our bodies clicked. I was taking care of him, and he was taking care of me. The surrender was total, and when we both came, the sound he made was coming from so deep within him, something I had never heard before. I latched on to him like I was never going to let him go. All I wanted to do was to stay there with him and not leave my room.

DOWNHILL

In the morning, he had to leave for work. I spent the day in bed, feeling abandoned and crying my heart out. I called my good friend Nelleke who had been my rock the previous year, and I couldn't even speak without bursting into tears. I had given up a piece of myself to him just to make it work.

From that moment, I worked hard on what was only the beginning of a relationship. Every time I was with him, I enjoyed it so much, but something was broken. I had made myself believe I couldn't be authentic or respect my boundaries in the fear that he wouldn't like me anymore once I did.

We saw each other at least once a week. We had dinner or sat on my porch, talking and drinking. He was so sweet, but if I was honest, I could feel he was pulling away. I didn't want to believe he was, counting the times we saw each other, rereading his texts constantly to assure myself it was only in my head and not based on reality. When I started with the waiting game of checking how long it would take for him to text me back, I was in complete agony. I would fall off the wagon and text him to get relief from the non-existent-but-oh-so-real prison I'd built for myself.

Our final date was at my house. Though we did the same thing we had done over the previous five weeks, having dinner and talking, the soul was out of it. We had a conversation but didn't connect. We had sex, but it felt empty. We cuddled, and it was what I needed so badly—him to hold me. I could feel the distressed inner child who finally had what it couldn't find anywhere else. Like the little light of a candle in the darkness. Something told me he needed it too, that inside of us there were two little children looking for a way to not feel alone. At that moment, he didn't feel like the man of my life, but I did make him the only man who could make me feel better.

We tried to see each other after that, but it never worked out. His work seemed to take up more of his time. Communication became scarce, and after a couple of more days, it stopped altogether.

Even though the reality of the situation was that he wasn't the man for me, I would have done anything to bring him back, to have him hold me and talk and have fun, like how it had been on the first couple of dates.

Instead, I felt darkness. I called him a couple of times and texted, but my worst fear had come to life. He fell off the face of the earth. I got dumped—without even hearing the words.

I saw him once more in a bar around the corner from my house. It was around midnight, and I felt drawn there. When I saw him at the bar, I went to talk to him immediately. I could tell he had been drinking for a while, and he looked surprised to see me. "This is awkward," I told him, my face must have had a mix of rage and fear because he didn't know how to react. Part of him looked happy to see me, and he kept on saying how we should see each other again soon. I left after only a couple of minutes because I felt horrible. I couldn't say what I was feeling or had felt, and he was drunk anyway, so there was no point in staying.

The next couple of weeks, my anxiety level was off the charts. On the one hand, I wanted to run into him once more, and on the other, I never wanted to see him again. He had been looking for a place in the neighborhood, and every time I opened my front door, I was scared I'd see his face.

31.
THE BLACK HOLE

Do you know the feeling when the ground under your feet is crumbling? You feel like you're falling, and nothing can stop you from crashing. It is often followed by a sea of tears that never bring relief. I had experienced this feeling before. When I got into a huge fight with a friend when we were traveling through Iceland and I couldn't stop crying for two days straight. Or when I was twenty-one and had to break up with my boyfriend even though I was still very much in love with him. When the handsome chef ghosted me after six weeks, it felt like all those previous tragedies, but more of an amalgamation of all the heartbreak I had felt before.

I sat in my apartment feeling a huge pit in my stomach. Not moving. Disconnected from everything around me. The living room was a mess, but I couldn't move or lift a finger to do anything about it. My stomach was feeling like one solid block of concrete, shifting up and down with every breath I took. The TV was on, but I was barely aware of the visual stimulation. It was just another form of intoxication. I was floating around, but not really there. I was not hungry, but I wanted to eat, drink, or smoke, anything to numb the pain. I spent hours looking at my phone, and it not ringing was the most deafening sound. I would scroll endlessly, swipe left or right, but never make any real connection. I would have a glass of wine or two or three. Nobody texted me, but I didn't want to reach out to anyone either. Instead, Instagram stalking, looking at pictures, reading texts over and over again—those were my default activities. There's something about grief that makes you want to disconnect from the world when all you need at that moment is connection. Hours passed like this, yet nothing would happen. No resolution. Not one glass of wine or piece of candy could pull me out of this state. Sometimes, I would fall asleep, which would finally mean the end of a particular episode.

I had fallen into a void. It seemed a matter of life or death, that I was not going to make it, as I grasped for every little branch I could hold on to. Hoping to get out. Hoping not to crash down even further inside the nothingness while constantly fighting. The odd thing is that there was never an actual crash. Maybe even worse than an actual crash—I was locked in this anti-state. A perpetual waiting-for-nothing paralysis where all the fibers in my body were amped up, and no relaxation was in sight. The energy was stagnant and stuck. There were no tears, for that would mean movement. Instead, a circling crawl into darkness. In the mornings, everything would feel better, and my behavior felt dramatic and out of proportion.

This pattern came up anytime my love was unrequited. It could go on for days, weeks, sometimes even months until the idea of that love would fade, or the joy of another man came in. It seemed like the source of all the discomfort was my not accepting the current state and, instead, trying to fight the situation, fighting my feelings and not being okay with how things were going. All the discomfort and agony seemed to stem from the disconnect between what I was feeling and how I wanted to feel. I made so many lists and plans, telling myself, "Next time I'll ..." and filling in that blank with any of the following: journal, meditate, turn off my phone and go for a walk, reach out to friends, dance in my apartment, or scream. But I always seemed to forget about all those good intentions. It was time to start genuinely connecting with myself.

32.
NO GUTS NO GLORY

With my thirty-first birthday approaching, an idea hatched and there was no way of stopping it. I had been confronted with my existential wound after the chef disappeared and had simultaneously started a new training, which brought up a lot. I had been writing and journaling more than usual, and one day at the beginning of August, I had the strongest urge to start a blog. For the first time in my life, I had felt an undeniable spark, like an idea was planted in my head that wasn't mine, but I had to follow through. It was 2016, and I'd completely missed the boat on this medium. By that time, it seemed like every housewife, ten-year-old, therapist, and schoolteacher had started a blog, and there didn't seem to be a need for new voices.

That weekend, my new roommate Annie and I were sitting at an Italian wine bar where we took up the only table on the terrace outside. Annie had always been passionate about language. She studied Germanic languages in Amsterdam and did an intense acting master's in the most renowned school in Belgium. We were brainstorming about what the blog could be called, and she came up with the name "beterbloot.com," which translates as "Better Naked." It was a bit quirky, intriguing, and interesting, and it felt right; I didn't want to consider anything else. From start to finish, it was an intuitive process, and everything came to me because it had no pressure to be anything else.

I didn't care that it was an antiquated medium. I had finally found my way of creating as an adult. I loved the process of writing the blog. I didn't do it to get anything in return or for it to be a success; I did it for me and by sharing my stories in a vulnerable way, I wanted to show women everywhere that they weren't alone and they didn't have to be ashamed even for their most embarrassing or dark stories. I wanted to provide a feminine support system, which we had forgotten we needed. I didn't get a large following at all, and it was mostly read by my friends, but it was so liberating.

I felt supported by my friend Eva who had moved to Amsterdam the same day as me. We were from the same region and hit it off immediately. She was a short, witty, inquisitive redhead and an editor at a publishing house. She and Annie had been proofreading everything I was planning to post. She questioned some of the blogs, whether I was sure I wanted to post about my daddy issues or my mother. She wouldn't dream about writing something like that about her family. She asked, "What if your parents read this?" I didn't even worry about it because I knew my family either wasn't going to read it, or if they did, they wouldn't say anything about it. It made me a little sad but also brought me some freedom. I had to tell my truth, whether it was pretty or not.

33.
HEART & SEXUALITY

The search for myself pushed me into new spaces. I had finished all the courses The School had to offer, but I was hungry for more. Some of the trainers had followed a course called Heart & Sexuality. It started as a way to help people reprogram themselves when it came to sex, which influences so many areas of our lives. Part of the process was to go back to some of the most critical moments in our sexual development and reprogram those key events with different exercises and roleplay. We didn't sit around and talk, but we used our bodies as we had done with Patricia. I was astonished about the amount of knowledge that was stored in our cells and could be accessed and transformed with the right guidance.

For the first time, there were men in the training, and it threw me off completely. I was used to developing myself in a safe space of women, and all the masculine energy took me out of my comfort zone. The course consisted of six four-day trainings that took place in the middle of nowhere in the Dutch countryside. It was a huge commitment, but I had managed to figure everything out at work, and I was ready even though I didn't fully know what I was getting myself into.

We were staying on a farm that had a converted barn where all our sessions took place. The main brick building was used for sleeping and eating. When I arrived there for the first time after a three-hour drive from Amsterdam, I felt so heavy. What had I gotten myself into? The entire first weekend, I was tired and couldn't really get into it. We had to do exercises with men, and I felt intimidated when I saw a guy in my group yelling his heart out in an exercise where the person in front of him was impersonating his ex-wife who had cheated on him. I remember seeking shelter with the women, and I started crying like a little girl when I was experiencing this surge of masculine anger coming at me. It reminded me of my childhood, when we were tiptoeing around my dad, trying not to make him go off and when he did, I had no defense.

Every weekend of the training tackled a different age range to heal, and when we got to adolescence, we spent four days being teenagers and breaking away from our parents. Mine hadn't tolerated teenage behavior. Everything was pretty serious in our house, and when my sister broke up with her first boyfriend after six months when she was sixteen, my parents were so upset. They told her there wouldn't be a string of boys coming around, and it stuck with me. Love was serious and not playful. In this safe space, I could go back to those teenage years and go role play with one person after another, not worrying about the consequences.

34.
DADDY ISSUES

One afternoon we came into the room to find they had put up mattresses in front of every person's spot. The exercise that day was to pretend the mattress was your parent. Up to this point, we had already done so many exercises with role play and props that this wasn't a foreign concept to me. The first part of the exercise was to tell our fathers what we had always wanted to say to them, what we missed, about specific events from our childhood, how we felt about them, and how much we appreciated and loved them. For the second part, we had to physically work out how we had felt about our father on the mattress. It could be kicking, screaming, hitting, yelling, or crying, anything our bodies were telling us to do. Whatever we needed to make all our frustration with our parents disappear. When they said we needed to do this for twenty minutes per parent, I didn't know where I would find the strength.

I hadn't had the best relationship with my father. It was not the worst either, but we definitely didn't have a strong connection up to that point. I didn't feel I could connect with my father. I always thought my behavior was disappointing to him and he thought I wasn't trying hard enough, and by default, I wasn't good enough for him. As a child, I was super social, I drew and sang all the time. He was a man who liked math and IT. I was late and chaotic, forgetting or misplacing a lot of my belongings; my dad was always on time and is still the most organized man in my life. Being his youngest daughter, I was told he had a soft spot for me, but I couldn't really feel it as a child. I didn't remember having that much interaction with him apart from schoolwork. Every time I would get a bad grade or lose my wallet or ID, I was so afraid to go home because he was going to be so disappointed and mad, and there would be a punishment involved. He didn't understand or condone my forgetful behavior.

My guess is he didn't see how I was ever going to get through the world, and he wasn't able to vocalize any of his worries or emotions; everything came out as orders or blame. He hadn't had the best childhood because my grandfather had a drinking problem and my grandma lost a baby when my dad was very young. He had to fend for himself emotionally from a young age. He had created a warm family around him by giving us hugs and showing my mom a lot of love, but words were difficult for my family, and nobody would share their deepest feelings at the kitchen table.

The first thing they ask in any self-development course is to look at your family and where you come from. My relationships with men hadn't been going the way I wanted, and I saw a correlation between how I had related to my father and how I related to men. I had put the stamp of emotionally unavailable on my dad, and that seemed a worthy explanation of my entire dating experience. I thought I was looking for my father's love in every man I dated. I got the idea that whenever I wanted love or recognition, I had to work incredibly hard to earn it, and I applied this to every area of my life. At work, it actually had brought me far, but in relationships, it messed me up. It was the textbook definition of daddy issues. For the past couple of years, I believed that the existential wound I had—or the sadness and blackness I felt—had to do with my father, and I was constantly looking for a better way to deal with it.

And at the retreat, I found myself standing in my leggings and hoodie looking at a mattress where I could unleash all the feelings I had been holding on to. The mattress leaned against the wall, so I could stand on my feet while I was going at it. It took me a little bit to get into it, but after a while, all the kicking and screaming felt like it was done by the four-year-old and the fourteen-year-old inside of me, who were letting go of everything that had been locked inside for all this time. Every single event, feeling, or frustration was released until my voice was gone, and I could barely lift my arms anymore.

35.
OUT OF MY HANDS

On the final day of the training, I woke up to an epiphany. I suddenly felt like I knew what had to happen, and it was, again, bigger than me and like my blog, didn't seem to be my idea.

You *must* move to Boston.

For the last three years, I had been working for my company in the European headquarters in the Netherlands. Our global head office was in Boston, but I had never felt the urge to move there. I could only do my dream job at the global headquarters, but I had never pictured myself living in the United States and especially not in Boston. That morning, in the countryside in Holland, I felt a huge impulse that it was time for me to move to America. It wasn't an aggressive feeling, and it didn't make me feel upset. It was more like a steady knowing that I couldn't ignore. I told Nelleke, "I guess I'm moving to Boston."

When I got back into the office after I had completed the course, I put everything into work. It seemed like I knew exactly what had to be done to reach my goal and put everything into place. I reached out to everyone I could think of in both Amsterdam and the United States, lobbying and asking for advice. In December, my boss was at headquarters in Boston, and he texted me that a job just opened up on the exact team I wanted to be a part of.

The night before my final round of interviews, Annabelle stayed over because her boyfriend wanted to watch the Superbowl, which was at 3:00 a.m. European time. She'd never spent the night at my apartment, and I forgot she was a light sleeper, and the tram passed by my house. I was used to it, but she didn't sleep a wink that night. I could feel her tossing and turning, and by default, I didn't sleep much either. I was so tired that morning and didn't have the energy to be nervous. I had prepared meticulously, and the four hours of interviews passed by in the blink of an eye. Interviews had never been my strong suit and nerves could overwhelm me, but I had been so tired that I could only answer the questions, and stress didn't overtake me.

I started interviewing at the beginning of January, and I knew I had the job by the end of February. I had never seen the universe deliver what I was asking for so quickly. Sure, I'd been dabbling in putting things out there and getting rewarded or lucky, as some of my friends would say, like with my apartment in Amsterdam or being able to find a parking spot in front of wherever I had to be. But getting the Boston job had been transformative. It felt like it had not been my wish, but that the seed had been planted in my head, and I was following the script. My ego had gotten out of the way on this one, so I couldn't ruin it by doing my best.

AYAHUASCA

Nelleke had been my biggest supporter throughout the past year. She was with me when I got the idea to move to Boston and during all the ups and downs of my dating life. She had become my confidante, and I felt comfortable being with her. At first glance, we weren't an obvious match since she was sixteen years older than me and a therapist with three children who were only a couple of years younger than me, but from the first moment we met, I picked her and knew she was going to be a close friend.

Once I knew when I was going to leave for the United States, she offered me an ayahuasca ceremony as a gift. I didn't know much about it, and I was intrigued. She had done one before with her husband, and she had gained huge insight. However, her husband hadn't been able to let go and give in to what the plants had to tell him. I didn't do any research at all, but the fact that Nelleke offered this to me was good enough to make me trust it was safe.

The last weekend of March, we were in the car on our way to a suburb of Amsterdam where we would do a ceremony of the sacred plant with eight other people. We had to fast the week before, which meant no coffee, no sugar, no meat, and no alcohol. That wouldn't have been a problem if it weren't for the suddenly gorgeous spring-like weather in Amsterdam that made me want to have a glass of rose outside for the first time in months. I felt the withdrawal of chemicals leaving my body. I had a drink with Eva the day before, and she couldn't stop laughing at my very unsatisfied face. We couldn't eat anything at all the day of the ceremony, so we were a little lightheaded when we stepped into the space on Friday evening. We were dressed in white, as instructed, and found the others in beautiful white outfits, welcoming us like old friends.

After everyone arrived, we gathered in a circle to share what had brought us there. Everyone had a story, and the group was very diverse. There was a young guy who was recovering from depression, a retired teacher and his wife who were looking for more meaning in their lives, and a gorgeous young couple who had come there to work through some of their issues since she had been raped years ago, creating a divide between them. He was a six-foot seven-en man of Indian descent, and she was a beautiful brown-haired Dutch woman with big blue eyes. Dressed completely in white, they looked like a dream. A screening had been done thoroughly by the people who organized the ceremonies. People couldn't be on any sort of drugs or have current psychological problems, and they could deny anyone at any point. It made me feel secure that all these people I was going to be sharing something life-changing with were meant to be there.

After the group sharing, we all were poured a small glass of tea, the ayahuasca, and they gave us a peppermint. I would very soon find out the mint was necessary because the potion tasted like a mix of cold bitter coffee and dirt. The couple who organized the session would function as modern-day shamans playing music and guiding us. We relaxed and lay down on our mattresses under our blankets waiting for something to kick in. They had already explained the different stages of the experience and gave us some advice about things we could encounter. If we seemed to be experiencing death, or someone dying, it would usually mean a new beginning, and their advice was to relax and lean into the experience. You could also always ask questions or demand clues to mother Ayahuasca and an answer would present itself.

I closed my eyes and tried to relax. Pretty quickly, I started to see wonderful colors, and it felt like I was descending into deeper layers of my consciousness. The visions were brightly colored, surprisingly symmetrical, and always in movement. I was perfectly aware of where I was and what was happening, and I even did a little test to see if the visions would still be there if I opened my eyes. The plant only worked inside of me, so I relaxed and let myself float away.

Every single man I had dated passed by in a herd, and when they turned around, their faces changed into Venetian masks, and they crumbled into pieces and fell down a ravine. I wasn't particularly sad when this happened. I shrugged and went on with my journey. A bit later they all came back, and this time they were dressed in black cloaks with red lining. I could see the last guy I had dated in Amsterdam, Max and Jacob, and even though I didn't recognize all of them, I knew they were there. Suddenly, I asked, "But what about the chef?" And immediately, I saw him appear as a tall, skinny figure dressed in white with extremely pale skin. The others had to help him walk and give him support like he was a fragile, old man, and immediately, I understood. He was too weak and couldn't give me what I needed. He wasn't ready for growth, and from that moment on, I could let it—and him—go.

I kept seeing my dad and even witnessed his death; I got overwhelmed by sadness, but I immediately remembered that it wasn't real and it was a new beginning. I felt the pressure on our relationship lifting and my daddy issues were starting to dissolve.

My niece kept appearing in my visions. I was her godmother, and I felt very connected to her. Maybe we had some shared experience, and maybe it had to do with her connection to her dad. I felt such a strong bond with her, and I thought coming out of this I needed to connect with her more. I kept seeing a little girl who looked like me, but everything around her was dark, and she was dressed in black. She was tiny, and looked at me with a mix of longing, anguish, and anger. I thought it was a representation of my inner child who I had been ignoring and was trying to build a relationship with for the last couple of months.

It was a journey I was on, and at the end of every act, I said, "Now I have to move forward." In the next chapter, I got to see my future, and two little girls with long curly hair appeared. They were smiling and holding each other's hands, and I instantly knew they were my daughters. I somehow also noticed that they were French; it all made sense. "Where is my husband?" I asked, and I felt his grounded presence behind me and knew it was right. Feelings of gratitude and contentment came over me. It would all be fine. It was the end of my first journey, and when it started to wear off, I felt like a goddess. Nelleke lay next to me, and all we could do was smile at each other.

37.
MISSING PIECE

It must have been around ten o'clock at night, when it was time for the second dose. We all got another little glass along with a peppermint, and I couldn't wait to go back to this amazing place where I could walk around and get all the answers and reassurance I needed. I drank the shot glass, leaned back, and waited for it to start working. The colors appeared, and I was going deeper and deeper, but the only thing I found this time was darkness. I started to sweat, my stomach was upset, and I grabbed the bucket that was next to me. It was so black that I couldn't see anything, and I started to panic.

Nelleke and I had made a promise to each other that we were each going to go on our journey. No taking care of each other, no being dragged out of the great consciousness and into each other's black hole. The two guides were there for that very reason, and when I felt I couldn't deal with it on my own, I called the two of them over, and the words, "You need to help me," came out of my mouth. They had told us that there was a possibility we would have an experience that felt close to death, and this felt like I was fighting for my life. I knew relaxing would make it go away, but no fiber in my body was willing to let go. People who drink from the plant often vomit even when they haven't had any food all day. How it was explained was that something old was leaving the body, and it usually had a very dark color.

This was all going through my head when I was trying to push it out of me, making myself puke out all the darkness. I kept on saying, "It's now or never, Fienie. You are here now; do your best, so you can spiritually move on." I usually couldn't throw up, only when there was too much alcohol involved. Even then, I could count the times it happened on one hand. Nothing helped, and it made me freak out even more. I was genuinely terrified. I kept calling the instructors over, and they were stroking my back. I especially needed the masculine power there to keep me grounded, to tell me it was going to be okay and I didn't have to face this ordeal alone. Alone being the key word, I felt alone spiraling in the dark. The entire session had been supported with music, and the atmosphere felt so ominous with the loud drums. It was like they were accompanying me down the rabbit hole, and I couldn't find my way out.

It went on for what felt like hours, and I knew the pushing wasn't working. I finally gave up and said to myself, "It just won't be for today." I curled up with the bucket in my arms and tried to relax. Immediately, I saw the little girl again who was surrounded by darkness. The words, "I have a sister," came to me. "I have a sister, and it's not the sister I know."

I instantly understood that this little girl in black was my twin. It was new information, and I had never heard anything about this, but every cell in my body knew it was true.

The shaman had explained how dead people could also surround us and use us as a gateway to leave and cross over. I hadn't paid much attention to this comment since it wasn't something that resonated with me, but lying there, I remembered. So much became clear; maybe it wasn't her who was using me to leave this world. Maybe I was fighting because I wasn't ready to let her go. Maybe it wasn't my dad who had put pressure on me to do my best, and I had just given myself that idea. Maybe I have always felt guilty that my body was strong, and I was the one who survived. Was the darkness that kept coming up the emptiness I had felt when she left me? Did the loneliness I felt since I was a little girl connect to her? Was this search for a partner trying to find the bliss I had felt in the womb? There were too many questions that I didn't have answers to, and when the effect started to wear off, all I felt was confusion. It was around two o'clock in the morning when the ceremony ended. I had some soup and bread before I went to bed to sleep it off.

In the morning, we had another sharing circle, and the stories were wonderful. The Indian guy had been reunited with his ancestors, and felt like he could finally understand where he came from. The most wonderful story came from his girlfriend who had seen that the man who assaulted her was in as much pain as she was, and if she didn't forgive him and let him go, they would be linked to each other forever.

She had seen his pain and could set them both free. They sat there, still dressed in white and absolutely glowing, like a king with his queen after winning the battle of a lifetime. Nelleke didn't have many words for what she had experienced, but she said she went as deep in the earth as she had ever been. When it was my turn, all I could say was that it was very heavy. I couldn't even share what I had seen, and I first had to process it myself.

PROCESSING

We drove back to Nelleke's house outside of Amsterdam where we sat on the couch drinking tea and wine all weekend while her husband took care of us. It was the grounding atmosphere I needed to help me process the experience. They had told us that the effect of the ayahuasca could go on for months, and things would start to fall into place. With the confusion I felt, I hoped it was true and the fog would lift.

The relationship I had with my dad changed immediately. A curtain had been lifted, and I could see that my entire life I had been projecting my fear and feeling of loss onto him. He probably had struggled with the same feelings when it came to his parents. However, I decided to stop the cycle. The realization that my twin had been the cause of my existential wound was still hard to process. What was I going to do with the information and was it even true? Even while I was questioning it, every cell in my body confirmed it and I couldn't ignore this feeling. I would have to let go of common-sense rationale and face that I got a piece of information that I never expected.

Later in the week I did some research on the topic, and I found the term "Vanishing Twin Syndrome." It is when one twin gets lost in the very early stages of pregnancy. It could be as early as six to eight weeks, and the effect on the other half is immense. People look for their missing part without even knowing what they are looking for. The statistics are through the roof. A book written by a team of gynecologists states that 10% of the population started as twins.

I needed some time to process all this information. I didn't want the Vanishing Twin Syndrome stamp because it felt like another means of victimhood and giving away my responsibility. I wasn't going to go around and say I was a vanishing twin survivor and have people see me as some sort of nutjob. On the other hand, it was such a relief knowing I hadn't imagined all this pain and other people have felt it too—that feeling of being alone and wanting to go back to the symbiosis I knew was there. I gathered up the courage to ask my mom if she had ever experienced bleeding at the beginning of her pregnancy and she had. She said the doctor never said she was carrying twins and she didn't resonate with the information I was giving her. But the fact she had experienced something that could explain all of it, confirmed what I already knew inside.

MOVING ON

The seance was a way to close out my three years in Amsterdam. Getting the visa for the United States took longer than anticipated, but after all the paperwork was done, I was ready to start the next chapter. Amsterdam had been everything I wanted, a town full of cool, progressive people. I needed a souvenir of the city I had loved so much, and on my last Sunday, hungover after one of my goodbye parties, I booked an appointment with a tattoo artist I knew to have the three crosses of Amsterdam's crest marked on my ankle. It was my proof. I was grateful for all of it, the experiences, the housemates, the countless nights at the kitchen table and the warmth they gave me. But I had to leave my Dutch family. Amsterdam was great, but not my final stop. For some reason, it felt like I needed an even more radical change, and I left for the United States at the beginning of summer.

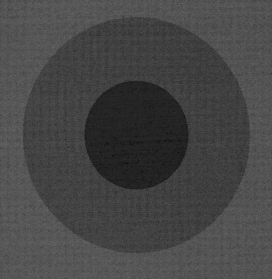

UNITED STATES
TRUE PURPOSE

40.
TIDAL WAVE

Uprooting and moving 3,500 miles away was the hardest thing I have ever done. It took me months to truly arrive mentally and emotionally. All my dreams were still taking place in Amsterdam or Belgium, and always ended up in my parental home. It was like I left a part of myself in Europe. I was adjusting to the different cuisine and gained more than ten pounds in the first couple of months. I remembered Patricia mentioned putting on weight was always about creating an extra level of protection. Maybe I needed that extra layer to get through this challenge. The first six months were a whirlwind. I had to get the lay of the land, explore my new city, get used to my new job, and find my tribe. I was staying in corporate housing again. The apartment was modern and had all the space and appliances I needed, but I didn't feel like the building had a soul. I knew I had to find a place with more character, so I could start feeling settled.

The search for my new apartment took three months. I found a lovely one-bedroom apartment near Back Bay, one of the most beautiful and historic neighborhoods in town. My new home was on the first floor of a one-hundred-year-old brownstone building. We had a little garden in front where we could hang out during the summers. I put all my crystals on the mantelpiece along with cards, figurines, books, pictures and the Buddha that Annabelle gave me. I was relieved I had found a place, and I couldn't wait to start decorating, something I had never cared about before. I frequented decorating stores for furniture, and when I was in a Dutch design store, my eye fell on a pink velvet couch. I felt like now would be my window if I ever wanted to have a light-fabric piece of furniture. Neither boyfriends nor kids would approve, so I had to go for it. This was the first time I had ever truly lived on my own without family or roommates, and my mission was to make my apartment as beautiful and cozy as possible.

Moving across the Atlantic also brought me a sense of liberation. No one would judge or scrutinize me simply because no one knew me. I could go wherever I wanted, spend as much money as I felt like, shift my view on things completely, change my behavior, and nobody would know the difference. I could reinvent who I was, and that presented so many new possibilities.

41.
NEW FAMILY

Ava, a colleague who moved from the UK office a couple of months earlier, took me under her wings when she found out I was moving to Boston. Ava and her husband John had both experienced what it was like to take a big leap and helped me anyway they could. Ava made sure to invite me to all the happy hours, dinners, or parties they were going to. They immediately felt like home. She introduced me to a group of colleagues she hung out with a lot including Christopher from Michigan, Frank from London, and Leyla from Germany.

Leyla had moved from Europe to the US with her family ten years earlier. She and her colorful, warm family invited their European friends who didn't have a family nearby for every holiday. They had an amazing house forty minutes outside of Boston, we called the compound. I got invited to Easter brunch, the Fourth of July, Labor Day barbecue, Thanksgiving dinner, and Christmas lunch with the group.

There was so much banter going on those days that I almost peed my pants from laughter at least once when we went over there. I was slowly building a life for myself with new friends, new habits and finding a new baseline. Being so far away from home made friends became more than just friends. The friends I chose to spend holidays with became family. Not the family you get by birth, but the one you choose. It made me feel more grounded– and I could use all the grounding I could get.

42.
THE VIKING

The first weekend of September, I was in New York to celebrate the fiftieth birthday of my good friend Ryan. He and I had worked together for over three years and had formed a strong connection. He had started a clothing brand together with his best friend, Richard that combined their two passions: denim and motorcycles. In a short period, they built a big following all over the world. They spent half the year traveling, going to fairs to promote their brand and meet aspirational retailers. Wherever they traveled, they surrounded themselves with artists, musicians, photographers, and creatives. The birthday party was going to be at a huge motorcycle fair in Brooklyn organized by a couple of their friends. It wasn't really my scene, but Ryan and I always had a lot of fun together, and I could appreciate the tall, bearded men who were going to be there. Ryan and Richard looked tough– covered from head to toe in tattoos and wearing rings, chains, and denim– but they were two sweet and loyal guys.

I arrived in the city on Friday night and met Ryan to drop my bags in Chinatown where we were staying. We went for ramen and sake around the corner from the loft with Ryan's friends who were hosting us. I could smell in the air that it would be a memorable trip. After dinner, we went to a party hosted by a biker magazine where we were going to meet Richard and some other friends. I walked in, and the first people we saw were a guy and a girl standing at the bar. The guy checked me out from top to bottom and his gaze made me feel very self-conscious and a little shy. It had been a while since a man made me feel like that. He was a big guy and was wearing off-white denim pants, a black t-shirt, and suede Red Wing boots. He had a blond buzzcut and wasn't objectively handsome, but the energy he exuded was very masculine, raw, and attractive—to me at least.

His name was Oscar and he was Ryan's Danish friend who had just got back from a week at Burning Man, the festival of self-expression in the Nevada desert. At first, I was a little intimidated, but since everyone was giving my friend shots for his birthday, I loosened up quickly, and it turned out to be a great party. Oscar and I talked for a while about his experiences with psychedelics that summer, and I shared a bit about my ayahuasca experience. Even though we had a great conversation, it was his energy that immediately impressed me. He told me he lived in Copenhagen, and his passion was boats. He already owned a wooden boat, but his dream was to buy an old ship and convert it into a houseboat. "You guys are standing awfully close to each other," said Richard, Ryan's best friend, winking at me.

The night ended abruptly when it was apparent that Ryan had had more than enough to drink. I didn't want to jeopardize the rest of his birthday weekend, so Oscar carried him into a taxi, and we headed back to Manhattan. Unfortunately, to get to our fabulous loft, we had to climb four flights of stairs. After a good thirty minutes, a lot of persuading, support, and motivating, we made it all the way up, and I put Ryan to bed.

We spent the next day at the motorcycle fair in Greenpoint. It was Ryan's fiftieth birthday, so there would inevitably be a party. When we were getting out of the Uber, the entire street was packed with rugged yet stylish men with long hair, beards, sunglasses, Red Wings, and special denim, looking at special motorcycles. We entered the hall and looked for the brand's booth. It was only three o'clock in the afternoon, but there was already a party vibe at the place. Some tattoo artists were putting little tags designed for the event, photographers were taking pictures on a professional set and bands were playing live music all day. Other brands were selling helmets, clothing, accessories, and magazines inspired by the subculture. We started with a beer, and Ryan immediately introduced me to new people. I started dancing to the music, and helped sell their gear even though it didn't seem like that was the priority of the day.

After a couple of hours, Oscar walked in wearing sunglasses. He didn't seem as intimidating as the night before, but I was still fascinated by his energy, deep voice, and disarming smile. We talked and bantered like we had known each other for years, but something about it felt brand-new.

When the VIP bar ran out of food, Oscar and I decided to go have dinner around the corner.

I found myself at a corner bar in Greenpoint having tacos and drinks with this guy and having more fun than I'd had on all the dates I'd been on in the past year. It felt effortless the way we were talking and laughing. I was enjoying how close I was sitting to him, looking into his blue eyes. By the time we got back to the event location, it was time to move the party somewhere else. He mentioned he was going to go meet a friend downtown, but I didn't pay too much attention to it. There was no doubt in my mind that he was coming to the party with us. When he left, he held onto my hand a bit longer than was deemed normal, and we stood there for what felt like the longest, quietest, most intimate, and suspenseful minute.

I left him there and walked out with Ryan and the crew. We had a couple of drinks at the bar down the street, and it was obvious everyone was in the mood. We had a group with Brazilians, Belgians, Danes, and Americans, who were all picking up on the vibe, and it seemed this night might turn into something momentous. I kept checking the door waiting for Oscar to walk in, but he didn't show up. I remembered that I had his number since Richard had used my phone to call him earlier, so I texted him. "I can't believe you left without saying goodbye!" No reply.

Had I misunderstood? Hadn't there been a vibe these past couple of days? Was I making too much of it? What was I even thinking or expecting anyway from a guy who lived in Copenhagen and just went to a crazy ten-day festival where he did God knows what and I had just moved to another continent?

The loud music, drinks, and company made me let it go. As per usual when Ryan and I went out, we had a blast. We had been friends for years, and our combo was a guarantee for a good time. We brought out the mischief in each other. The night brought us to many different places across Brooklyn. We had a photobooth moment, I was dancing wearing someone else's hat for most of the evening, and I had meaningful conversations with an older Brazilian gentleman who didn't speak English very well but had a big heart and the biggest bag of coke I had ever seen.

We ended the night at five o'clock in the morning at the loft of Ryan's friends. We first had to wait outside the door for fifteen minutes, scared to wake everyone up because we were laughing so hard about something that we couldn't remember the next day. When we finally went in, we found Ryan's entire bedroom filled with colorful balloons. Trying to make your way through a room full of balloons when the sun is coming up, you had too much to drink and can't wait to go to bed is not ideal. We spent Sunday sleeping in, having brunch, hanging out in Chinatown, and by 5:00 p.m. I headed over to Penn Station, ready to take the train back to Boston. Ryan told me that Oscar had been hanging out with Richard and his girlfriend and they asked if we could meet up, but I didn't feel like seeing them. The moment had passed and the weekend was over.

I had only been on the train for half an hour when I got a message from Oscar. He was on his way back to the airport after three weeks in the US and had to go straight into work the next day. We talked for a couple of hours while he was getting ready to board, and it felt nice and relaxing. The usual internal chaos I experienced after meeting someone wasn't there, and I was at peace getting to know someone I probably would never see again.

43.
CONNECTED

Starting that Sunday, Oscar and I texted every day and over the next couple of weeks. our contact intensified. I wasn't really considering this thing becoming more than it was because there was an ocean between us, but I was absorbed by the connection, consumed with it, I felt sensations I had never experienced with anyone before. I wasn't thinking about the future simply because there couldn't be one, and it took the pressure off. We only held hands in New York, that made it feel very pure. I was simply getting to know him, and my energy was slowly connecting to his. My lack of steep expectations allowed something to develop without me realizing.

I shared many of my deepest thoughts with him, thoughts that I had never shared with a man. It felt different. He made me feel like a woman, something I hadn't experienced in a relationship. Being in that soft energy felt so good but also extremely vulnerable. I couldn't use my usual masculine energy to control the situation and that was new and frightening.

Since I moved to Boston, I found that distance didn't mean you could not be connected to the people you love. The distance deepened the true connections and allowed me to let go of the ones that weren't naturally bubbling up to the surface. The only way I could describe the connection to Oscar was like I could feel an invisible cord or channel from my heart to his reaching across the ocean. "It's going to sound weird, but it feels like I can feel your heart all the time, even when we're not talking", I told him. "That's not weird at all," he replied.

44.
PANICKING

Meanwhile I was immersing myself in American culture, exploring my new country. I was under the impression I was going on a trip to California at the end of October, but I had the timing all wrong, and ten days later, I found myself on a flight to Las Vegas. I would join Lucie for a week, exploring Joshua Tree National Park and chilling by the pool in Palm Springs. She had been traveling with Meredith, a girl I knew from Belgium, and I would join them for the final leg of their trip.

When I arrived, they were holding a handwritten cardboard nameplate, and the tone was set for our girls' road trip through California. We spent our first three hours walking around Vegas, having a drink and a bite to eat. I smoked a cigarette inside Caesars Palace just because I could and lost twenty dollars to a slot machine. The three-hour drive to our motel in Joshua Tree showed me the opposite of what I had observed in Vegas—pure, beautiful, and raw nature. It was only a preview of what we would see in the next couple of days.

Oscar and I were texting back and forth. Every day, he asked me how the trip was going, and when pictures went on social media, he was the first one to like or comment. It made me stare at my phone and crave the connection, and when the text or question didn't come, it would leave me out of alignment thinking about what was going on in Copenhagen. Somewhere, a hint of my insecurity found its way back into my body, infesting the new and pure thing. I was scared that my anxiety would come up again, and with that, I knew it already had.

Joshua Tree was magical. I expected elves and trolls to pop up from behind a rock any minute, and the sky was made of candy floss. Only in the US had I experienced such vastness of nature. It made me feel humble and connected to nature, but in some moments, I was still drawn to the world only unlocked by my phone. I would feel great and suddenly would look at the screen, wishing Oscar would check in.

After three days in nature, our next stop was Palm Springs. We were staying at the Saguaro Hotel, a contemporary, colorful, and quirky hotel where we spent the entire first day by the pool, swimming, ordering drinks, talking, and reading. In the evening, we were going to meet some Belgian friends who were staying at the Ace Hotel a couple of blocks away. After our pool day, we showered, dressed up, and landed in one of the coolest hotels in the city.

The guys we had dinner with were doing a similar California road trip as us. They were also on the last week of their trip and thought they needed one more party before going home. As a result, the rate at which they were ordering bottles of wine at dinner was not slowing down, and we were getting wasted at breakneck speed. I enjoyed speaking Dutch a lot. Since arriving in the US, I hadn't found anybody in Boston who could speak my mother tongue. I got talking with one of the guys, and as the night progressed, we kind of hit it off. We went from the pool to their room and one thing led to the other. We ended up making out and fooling around. At that point I didn't know where my phone was, and I wasn't thinking about any of the consequences. After jumping in the pool one more time, we walked back to our hotel. All three of us fell asleep immediately.

The morning was a rude awakening. Why did I make out with this guy if my heart was saying something else? The alcohol had a different plan, and I would have done anything to take it back. When we woke up, we had to pack because we were checking out at 11:00. My phone rang, and Oscar's picture popped up. I wanted to cry when I saw his name, and I was so relieved to hear his voice calling me babe. It felt like everything was going to be fine. I was trying to convince myself I didn't owe him anything, and I didn't know if I would ever see him again. While I was making my way back to Boston through LA, I tried to make myself believe it hadn't been a big deal and my chances with Oscar hadn't been wasted. Years before this would have messed me up, and I would have felt guilty for months. Now, I could just assess the situation and observe the reality. We were only getting to know each other and weren't officially dating, but somewhere I knew I was trying to deal with the stress that came with meeting a guy I had deep feelings for.

The weeks progressed, and Oscar and I still talked every day. I started to really want to see him again and was thinking of a way to make that happen. Dropping hints and looking at flights had been my only ammunition. I asked him the barely hypothetical question if I could come see him in Copenhagen, and he said he didn't know where this was going, but he would love to spend a couple of days with me. I was too impatient to wait for him to come up with the plan, so I tried to regain control of the situation and convince myself it was a good idea. I had waited for two months and longed to see him again. I thought I was playing it cool and said I would think about it, but every bone in my body was screaming, "Yes!" I booked the flights, and on Thanksgiving, I was on my way to Denmark.

LONG DISTANCE

While I was packing my bag for my Copenhagen trip, I called Gabrielle. She was one of the friends where our bond seemed to get more intense even though we were far apart. She became my soulmate and I felt like I could talk to her about everything. We would spend hours on the phone discussing everything about our lives. She was always the one to see romance in anything, and whenever I met someone, she often hoped, even more than me, that it would be the one. She had been with her husband for over ten years, and they were a couple I looked up to. They seemed to be evolving together while raising their two beautiful boys. I told her how nervous I was, and we went over what I would do or say when I arrived. If it didn't work out, I would go to my Danish friend Nora's house and cry on her couch. I had arranged for Oscar and me to have dinner with her and her husband, so she could give me her point of view.

I had been longing for the moment the plane touched the tarmac for weeks, but for some reason, I felt like I needed more time. The stress was running through my body.

Two days earlier, I confessed to Oscar that I was feeling nervous, and he said he felt it too.

I went to the bathroom and put my face on. I was going to look the best I could, and I didn't want him to be disappointed after he had been dreaming about me for the last two and a half months. I finally felt like I could leave the comfort of the ladies' room, so I turned my phone on. He had texted "2 min away." I couldn't believe it! In a minute, I would see the guy I had been yearning for since the day I met him. I would know at the first moment if I was still into him or not, or if I was just so intoxicated on bikers that it had all been an illusion.

46.
MOMENT SUPREME

I was standing at Starbucks when he came through the door. He was still as tall and attractive as I imagined. He gave me a big hug, took my suitcase, and said, "The taxi is waiting for us outside." He led the way, and I got in the black Mercedes that was parked in front of the airport.

All I could think about was holding his hand. This simple gesture calmed my entire nervous system, and it set the tone for the weekend. It was seven o'clock in the morning when we drove from the airport into the city, the roads were empty, and we barely talked, only glanced at each other, smiled, and held hands.

We dropped my bag off at his apartment and went for breakfast. It was a place where he was a local. It had a cool vibe, and the guy who ran the coffee bar was a tall, gray-haired, bearded guy who also was a part of the biker scene. Oscar's friends were coming in for their morning coffee, and I immediately got introduced to them. Everyone seemed to know who I was and what I was doing there. The guys were asking me questions, but I could hold my own. It might have been a test, meeting his friends for the first time early in the morning. Or maybe he was giving me a taste of what his daily life looked like since friends were a huge part of it.

We went back to his apartment after a couple of hours, and it felt like it was already late, but it was only ten o'clock in the morning. We laid down on the couch, and I was getting tired, but I knew that I wouldn't get to sleep immediately. I was anticipating our first kiss. He leaned over, and we started making out. We touched very slowly and curiously. There was no rush. After almost three months, it didn't feel like we had to rush. We got to a point where we moved to the bedroom and again gently and slowly, we were exploring the way intimacy was going to go for us. The contact we had the past couple of months had been loving and more than friends, but never sexual, so I had no idea what to expect.

We didn't get out of bed until it was already dark in Copenhagen, around 4:00 p.m. The weekend was filled with friends, and it felt like he had everything planned out. He took me out on his boat around the city, and we passed by the opera building and the old harbor. It was so cold, even with all my layers, that he ended up giving me his jacket. I felt so happy, with my Viking on the water. I felt lucky walking with him around the city, this big man who could take care of me and wanted to pay everywhere we went. I didn't need a man to pay for my meal, but since I had learned in The School that a man likes to do stuff or give things to show he cares for you, I had begun to receive and enjoy it more than I had anticipated. It was interesting that from the moment I had decided to give it a try, there had only been men who liked to offer me things crossing my path.

On Saturday, we met my friend Nora and her husband for dinner and drinks in the meatpacking district, one of the coolest parts of the city. The first bar we went to, was a very cozy local place that served traditional open sandwiches and was decorated colorfully. Ryan was my only friend who had met Oscar, and I was curious to see how this would go. Nora and Oscar hit it off, and it was nice to discover he didn't need to be taken care of, and I could take him absolutely anywhere. After my relationship with Jacob, I had put it on the top of my list as a nonnegotiable. In conversation, he said, "Can you believe this one flew all the way over here just to see me?" like he couldn't believe his luck. After dinner, we went out just the two of us, and I caught him taking pictures of me. I had forgotten the feeling of liking someone who liked me back. The night ended at 2:00 in the morning, and we biked all the way home.

On Sunday we slept in and went from the bedroom to the couch and back, ordered Thai food, and watched a TV show all afternoon. I couldn't remember a day where I felt more safe and at ease than that one. I was wearing his sweatpants, but I had never felt more feminine. Even though we didn't do anything notable, it felt like one of the best days of my life.

The final evening, we had dinner at an Italian restaurant not far from his old apartment. I dared to talk about what my plans were at the end of the year. I was working at the Amsterdam office the week before Christmas and was going to Belgium to see my family. Halfway through dinner, I built up the courage to ask him, "Would you like to come to see me in Amsterdam before Christmas?"

He smiled and said, "Of course, I would love that."

47.
DIFFERENT STAGES

Two days after I got back to Boston, Oscar texted me a picture of his ticket to Amsterdam. I was sitting on my pink couch and immediately burst into tears. *Did he just buy a ticket to come to see me?* The little girl inside of me couldn't believe someone would go through all this trouble just to see me, even though the adult woman did.

Oscar and I stayed in my old room in Amsterdam that had been converted to a music studio. I was so grateful that I could share the space that I had lived in for three years. When I was waiting for him at the airport, my heart was beating out of my chest. He was a bit delayed, which gave me even more time to get worked up. When he walked out of the airport, I continued to feel off-kilter. It took me a minute to get used to him being there. My tactic of kissing him and letting him hold me calmed me down a little. We went for dinner at one of my favorite restaurants in east Amsterdam. Throughout the night, I continued to feel a bit nervous, there were a couple of silences, which years ago would have got me spinning from anxiety, but with him, it was okay. I wanted him to meet more of my friends. He made jokes with Annabelle and brought gifts for my old roommates. They had never seen me with a guy I dated, because I had never arrived at that stage, but they loved the way he treated me.

48.
CRACKS

During the weekend, Oscar mentioned once or twice that he missed me so much when we were not together. I felt the same but could tell there was more behind his words. All weekend, we hadn't talked about when we would see each other next. He traveled a lot for work, but not many of those trips were close to the northeast of the United States. By that point, I felt so in love that I would do anything to make it work. When we went to bed the last evening, he started the conversation with, "I don't know how I'm going to do this." He mentioned once again that he already missed me so much, but he'd already planned a couple of long trips, including another Burning Man. He told me that he didn't want to change any of his travel plans and he didn't know when he would see me again. In short, he was saying that what we had was casual and that he wasn't going to go out of his way to see me.

If I hadn't been lying in bed, the ground would have sunk from under me. A rush of despair went through my entire body. Had I again arrived at the point where I was being abandoned? Dumped? I thought I had done everything right this time. The only thing I could say, while I was bawling my eyes out, was, "If you know you're going to break up with me, just do it now."

He seemed in shock about my reaction, he hadn't anticipated the conversation was going to go this way. He tried to comfort me, but I was inconsolable. He kept saying, "I like you and you like me, so there is no problem."

There were only tears that night. I held on to him for dear life, and he to me. That was maybe the last time I would be in his arms. We had to get up at 5:00 to get to the airport, and on the way there, it was all love and sadness. We stood there for what felt like hours hugging, kissing, and crying at the departure hall.

That morning, he'd said, "I would have gone with you to visit your family if you would have asked."

I wanted to believe it. He was a boy who wanted to be with me but wasn't ready to make any commitment.

49.
PARTING WAYS

My visits to Belgium around the holidays were usually one big Christmas dinner, and I wasn't feeling balanced, which didn't help. Oscar and I still talked, but I was so afraid it was going to fade out again. I still hadn't explained to him how anxiety could hit and where it came from. I was so scared to tell him. I was still making peace with whether I would accept what was shown to me during the ayahuasca, let alone explaining it to the boy I really wanted to like me. I wanted him to see me as a chill girl, but I couldn't accept that I wasn't.

At the beginning of January, a massive snowstorm hit Boston, and no flights could leave or come into the city. My flight got canceled two days in a row and after the second cancellation at midnight, I got a brilliant idea. It was more the way to instant gratification. I called Oscar and proposed that I would make a pit stop in Copenhagen on the way home. The man, bless him, said it was a great idea, but I could feel he wasn't feeling it. At that time, he was coming off ten days of partying in Ireland, and the reality of the

New Year and his everyday life had kicked in. He wanted to get settled, so my visit for a few days wasn't ideal.

I wasn't being true to myself either since I was making him the fix for my anxiety. I was going there to be close to him and realized that at the same time I was driving him further away. Even though people were calling me his girl-friend, which was music to my ears, I knew it wouldn't last, and I would have to face it soon.

50.
THE BLACK HOLE 2.0

January was rough and contact with Oscar was scarce. I gave him time to process, but the silence was deafening. The entire month felt cold, dark, and like once again I was surrounded by darkness. I was reading the book Lucie had given me for Christmas, *Return to Love* by Marianne Williamson. She wrote about how no matter the darkness we find ourselves in, we are always connected to everything and everyone around us.

In the state I was in, I didn't feel connected at all—to anyone or anything in my life. Even though I was going through something that would take me a while to get over, it felt slightly less dark than with the chef. My friend from The School in Belgium offered a different perspective, "Maybe you shouldn't call it the black hole. Maybe it's not black at all. Let's call it pink since you are sitting on your pink couch!" At least she made me laugh.

At the start of February, I called him and verbally communicated the obvious fact that we were over. I was nervous, and when he picked up the phone, I cut to the chase. He replied, "We don't have to talk about it now," to which I insisted, "But, Oscar, we do." He explained he was stressed about life and had so much stuff to take care of this year and that he didn't have the brain space to be in a mega long-distance relationship. I didn't know if it would have been the best for me either, but I would have done it anyway. It was the night of the Super Bowl and after some pondering, I went to see the game at my neighbor's apartment with Ava and John. I sat with her dog on my lap for most of the game. It was like she knew.

In a way, I felt like I'd lost something, but another part of me felt relief. I was out of limbo and could move forward away from the Viking. The difference with the chef was that Oscar hadn't broken my heart. It simply didn't work out. The experience was beautiful and showed me how deeply I could connect to someone.

51.
VISION FOR THE FUTURE

I decided to go to a new moon workshop in a yoga studio nearby to get out of my funk. A bubbly yoga teacher was hosting it. We first did some exercises to get out of our heads before we were prompted to build a vision board of what we wanted to evoke in our lives for the new month. The time frame wasn't too intimidating, so I didn't have the feeling I had to fit everything I wanted onto the piece of paper in front of me. It became an intuitive exercise, just cutting out inspiring pictures and phrases I came across and arranged them onto the page. The activity reminded me of the hours of crafting I did when I was a child while singing along to the songs on the radio.

The workshop was a nice chunk of time where I didn't think about Oscar, black holes, or heartache. I wanted to share this with some of my girlfriends, and the next couple of months, on the new moon, I invited them to my house, provided a home cooked meal, and afterward, we sat quietly on the floor of my apartment, listening to music and thinking about what we wanted to manifest for the next month. Some of the girls had wonderful results. New jobs, raises, new houses, and roommates were manifested. I didn't feel like I manifested a lot of concrete things, but my boards were always filled with groups of women in inspiring locations. Spending time with women was exactly what I needed to recharge my battery, nurture my soft side and reenergize.

At work, I was also surrounded by women. We were creating women's products and the entire team was female except for one male designer who had a very developed feminine side. My boss was a wonderful English woman who gave me the confidence and guidance I had been looking for. Alexa was the associate of our team, and after working together for a year, she had become my ride or die. We knew exactly how each other functioned, and we had each other's back. Throughout my career, I experienced how deep the bond with colleagues could be. It didn't fit my personality to have a clear distinction between my personal and professional life, so some of my colleagues became my favorite people.

52.
NOT OVER

I had kind of picked things up again with a guy I knew previously because he felt familiar and I needed safety after Oscar. But whenever I would hang out with him in those first six months after Oscar and I broke up, I would wake up and have a text from Copenhagen. Every. Single. Time. It was like Oscar felt he had to reach out or post something on social media to feel that our connection was still there. I had never been so connected with someone from so far. I knew he wasn't waiting for me, but what we had felt intense and I wondered when it would fade away. "You guys never have a normal conversation," Ava would say after heart emojis would come my way, and we both said we missed each other.

I needed something else to focus on. Traveling was bringing me so much joy, not only exploring new cities or countries, but also just the traveling itself. The lost time at the airport or on the plane and the hopeful waiting to arrive at a destination that might change my life forever, led me to plan a trip every single month. I recorded it on my social media with the hashtag #onetripamonth. People asked me how that was even possible and how I could take off so much time, but it was more a mindset I was bringing into my life. I took short trips to New Orleans; Portland, Maine; and New Hampshire. I took longer trips to Miami and Los Angeles, but I also got lucky to visit Paris, London, China, and Japan for work. I had to turn my attention away from Oscar and start concentrating on what I loved and what would bring me joy. I wasn't ready to face the fact that maybe I was running away from Boston, a city where I wasn't able to put down roots.

53.
NEXT CHAPTER

Even though I was still going through a rough patch, I thought I should get back on the horse and try dating again. My colleague would say to me, "I am so jealous you get to date and have men take you out in a city you don't know that well yet. It's amazing!" That was a fresh way of looking at it. I usually looked at it like torture, but I was willing to try this new perspective.

I was dating to make myself feel better and to feel a connection, get affection, or feel special. but I didn't know what I was looking for. After a slew of dates with guys I wasn't interested in, I had to say no to all of them. I always wanted to protect their feelings, but I couldn't fool myself anymore. I sent a lot of texts that read, "I had a really good time, but I don't think this is going anywhere." The universe wanted me to know for sure that I wasn't settling. The years after I broke up with Jacob, I had believed someone was better than no one, but I was slowly letting go of that limiting belief. I had to cut some cords with the men I had loved, especially Oscar. I couldn't keep all these threads and wrap myself in a cozy blanket of melancholy and possibility. I didn't need them anymore. Travel kept me going and put me in a consistent state of flow. I spent the new year with friends in South-Africa, traveled to New Orleans for a bachelorette party and Ava and I spent 24 hours in New Hampshire to celebrate her birthday.

54.
PARADIGM SHIFT

Then the pandemic hit. The day the office closed, I had to leave for Mexico to renew my visa. It could only be done abroad and couldn't wait any longer. It seemed like mission impossible, but I received the necessary stamps and paperwork the day before all American Consulates closed until further notice. Borders were closing every day and I got out after seven days of what would normally be a two-week trip. The world was shutting down and I was relieved to get back to Boston and quarantine as long as needed. For the first eight weeks, I was happy to be home. For once I enjoyed staying in one location instead of moving every couple of weeks. My days were filled with work and back-to-back Zoom meetings. After that, I'd try to go for a run, walk or bike ride, which sometimes worked and sometimes didn't. I attempted a variety of recipes and magically could find everything at the fully stocked local grocery store. I tried not to buy into the deep, collective surge of lack and hoarding but I did engage in drunk Zoom calls with friends in different time zones, watched all of Netflix, fostered a cat named Chloe for a couple of months, and had a few pointless video dates. My sleep was deep, and my dreams were extremely vivid. I was processing everything that had been locked inside for the past couple of decades and random people who I hadn't thought of in years popped up in my dreams.

After three months, I was over it. I had processed everything and the four walls of my apartment were starting to close in on me. I felt lonely and craved contact that did not come through a screen. I went for walks with friends and I formed a bubble with Noelle and her husband Sam. Noelle and I were colleagues and had bonded after arriving in Boston around the same time. On the weekends, I would bike across town to have drinks at their apartment and play with their adorable, fluffy Australian Shepherd.

During one of those cocktail hours, we hatched the idea of spending the summer somewhere else. It was unnatural for me to be in Boston this long and I needed new surroundings. We were not going back to the office soon and we wanted to enjoy what could be the last couple of months of working from home. Sam had a network that stretched across every corner of the United States, and it was only a matter of time before he would find us a refuge we could drive to that had high-quality wi-fi, an ocean view, and separate bedrooms and bathrooms.

A couple of weeks later, he called me and said he had found us a place in Wilmington, North Carolina that matched our needs. The pictures looked fine, and we could see the ocean, so I said it was good enough for me. In early

July, we packed up the car with all our luggage and the puppy and drove for two days through the countryside, watching nature change and stopping at all the vegan junk food places Sam had picked out along the way. We listened to podcasts in the car, Noelle and I took turns driving, while Sam took care of the dog. I felt like I was let out of a cage after being locked up for months. I could finally breathe again. When we arrived, it was clear the photos hadn't done the place justice. It was a brand-new apartment with three full bedrooms and a full view of the ocean from anywhere inside. My bedroom was at the front of the building and for the next two months, I would fall asleep to the sound of the waves. After living in a city for the last decade, I wasn't aware I needed it so bad. Wilmington was a little boho beach town with a university, and lots of creative spirits flocked there. Bella, who owned the place, had moved there from LA a couple of years before and had completely fallen in love with it. She had set up her pottery and real estate business and was planting some roots in the little town.

All of Sam's friends there were creative entrepreneurs. They created jewelry and art, they sold records, books, and vintage carpets, and they showcased their creations in their studios, at small markets and cute bars all over town. Throughout the summer, we got to know all of them while hanging at someone's house, swimming in the ocean, giving each other lessons in surfing, or exploring all the restaurants and bars with outdoor seating. On my birthday, we pulled oracle cards with the girls. It was a habit I picked up over the years and it was the easiest way to dig into what was going on below the surface. They shared what was going on in their lives and what their dreams were. Their lifestyle was very different from mine in Boston. It was more relaxed and felt freer. It made me wonder if this could be my future too.

The entire summer I focused on friendships, and relationships had took a backseat. Oscar was still entering my thoughts from time to time, but I was so done with being hung up on him. I could go to his Instagram profile with my eyes closed and I needed to do something. One afternoon, while we were lying on the carpet of the living room, Noelle helped me block his profile, delete all of our threads and erase his number from my phone. It was an act purely for me and not to evoke any reaction. If he needed to reach me, he would find a way. It was time I closed the chapter once and for all.

Noelle and I spent hours walking the beach in the evenings and on the weekends, discussing how this strange time made us think about what our plans were and how we could move closer to our most authentic way of living. Noelle had been promoted, and we discussed at length what she wanted her leadership style to be. I had been doing my job for more than four years and I had been trying to figure out what my next step was. Throughout my entire career, I had always known what I wanted to do next, but this time nothing was coming up. I was listing my values and ranking them, putting more time and energy towards the beliefs that were on top of my list, focusing on the female consumer, sustainability and self-development, but there didn't seem to be a next dream job popping up. Thankfully, the fact that my job was now remote opened up opportunities for a life of travel, driving around the country, and being free of a fixed location.

I didn't want to leave. Rather, I didn't want to go back to the city. We extended our trip week after week, and I felt much more at home in Wilmington than I ever had in Boston. I couldn't see myself sitting alone in my apartment, for God knows how long, until we were allowed to go back to the office. Being so close to nature in an inspiring atmosphere made me see options I hadn't seen before. My lease was up in September, and in the final week of August, while we were enjoying the last of the North Carolina scenery, I gathered up the courage to call my landlord to give up the lease. I didn't have a plan yet, but the pandemic had its own timeline, and I was going to enjoy the fact that we could work from anywhere for as long as I could.

55.
TAKEOFF

We returned to Boston before Labor Day, and I started clearing out my place right away. The energy felt heavy when I entered, something I hadn't sensed before, but it confirmed my decision that I had to go. Everything I had gathered over the years was wearing me down. Working in fashion for over a decade had filled up my wardrobe and shoe closet, and I had to get rid of it all. I sold all my furniture online, and as strangers picked up piece after piece my apartment was getting emptier every day. John helped me take everything that was left to charity. I put a couple of boxes of memorabilia and art in a friend's basement, and the rest in the back of my rental car.

I set sail for Maryland where I was going to stay with my good friend Katy in her father's river house. She and her sisters had fled there on the very first day of the lockdown. I had to process the fact that I had just canceled my apartment and what was left of my possessions could fit into a few boxes. I felt like I was living in a sorority house, but with Katy's dad who was equally part of the group. Katy and I worked on the same team, so we had a lot of meetings together and could prepare before and after our Zoom calls. After work we would go kayaking, do yoga or take some sort of workout class. On weekends, we would go out on the boat, cook, go on long walks, or have friends over and hang out in the garden. I felt part of the family but spending time with people came with its own challenges. I had been so used to living alone that I had forgotten about my people-pleasing coping mechanisms. Now was the time to apply all that I had learned in love and practice it in all my relationships. Being around people didn't mean ditching myself.

After six weeks the wanderlust kicked in and North Carolina was on my mind. I had embraced beach life that summer and I craved to be close to the ocean, hearing the waves crash. I said goodbye to Katy and her family and after spending a week in Virginia Beach, I drove down to North Carolina to spend time with the crew at Bella's wonderful house by the water. Nobody could go home for the holidays or have family fly-over, so we spend the day trying everyone's favourite recipes and drinking wine.

Because I was on a work visa, leaving the country was out of the question, so Noelle and Sam decided to drive down to North Carolina to pick me up and spend the holidays in Florida. It was the first time in my life not celebrating Christmas with my family and I had never realized that I needed this ritual since it had always been a given. We were in Saint Pete's for Christmas and on December 24th, we dressed up and enjoyed a full feast. After New Year's we drove down to Miami to meet other friends. We all had to get back to work, but the mild climate and our after-work activities kept us in a constant holiday mindset. Skipping the Boston winter was a not-so- small added bonus.

The second week of January, they all had to return home. I looked at flights to cities on my bucket list, but I couldn't decide where I wanted to go next. While we were in the car driving to the airport, I decided to stay in Miami and booked a room in a converted hotel that had a coworking space, a pool and a reasonable rate.

56.
ELLA AND THE GANG

After spending a month with friends, I appreciated the time on my own. I still sometimes got dragged into what the group was planning to do and if I didn't take time to think, I crossed my boundaries quicker than I realized. I was looking for some balance in my new lifestyle. For me it wasn't just a trip where I could go nuts and afterward go home and recharge. For the time being, I was a nomad and I needed some grounding, a foundation I could fall back on whenever I needed it. My morning practice was becoming increasingly important to me. I had been meditating for years and was trying out journaling as a centring practice, dancing, or whatever new spiritual habits I felt compelled to try. I had trouble maintaining a healthy diet because cooking in the communal kitchen wasn't appealing in pandemic times and I was surrounded with a huge spread of takeout options. Doing ten thousand steps a day or swimming one kilometer was my attempt to create an exercise routine when everything was in constant flux.

My plans were still vague and I was far from ready to go back. I enjoyed the road trip vibe, but I wanted more freedom when it came to transportation. I had been renting cars or riding with Noelle and Sam, but I was ready for a more long-term solution. A couple of years before, Alexa and I went to Los Angeles for work, and after an upgrade on the rental car we drove the streets in a bright-red, four-door Jeep Wrangler. We laughed the entire time, and after I got back to Boston, I started seeing Wranglers everywhere. Every time, it brought back the same feeling of freedom and adventure, and it became the symbol of what my life could be like. So my first and only stop was the Jeep dealership. I tried out a couple of different models, and I chose a cool, gray four-door model that was only a year old. I had never made such a big purchase, but I felt in my bones that it was right. I could see myself continuing my travels with this new partner. I didn't grow up valuing material things, and I experienced guilt whenever I splurged on nice clothes or beauty products, but this time I set the guilt aside. The feeling I got when I sat in that jeep, imagining I was exploring the continent, trumped all the old limiting beliefs. Sold.

After a couple of weeks, I needed more social contact than I was getting. I enrolled in a full-moon kayaking class followed by a bonfire with wine and s'mores about a thirty-minute walk from the hotel. While we were on the water, I spotted three girls who looked about my age and were having lots of fun. That evening, by the fire, I sat next to Isabelle, a Colombian Capricorn who had moved to Fort Lauderdale three years earlier. Communication went smoothly and just like that, we planned to hang out the upcoming week.

That Saturday, we went for dinner and stopped by the pool party at the hotel. We ended up one block away at an outdoor bar with great music. A guy chimed in, speaking to us in broken English. He had arrived from Argentina a week earlier. Even though there was a language barrier, we communicated on a level that transcended words. In the following weeks, the three of us spent hours at the beach, danced at more pool parties at the hotel and drove around the Keys one weekend, a peninsula on the southern tip of Florida and the southernmost point of the United States. I had traveled solo before, but ahead of every trip the extrovert in me still felt some anxiety about not getting enough social contact and ending up having more alone time than I preferred. Encountering these lovely humans made me believe that when I followed my gut, inspiring people would cross my path. We also named the jeep Ella, a name that had a strong presence in my life. It was clear she would be my loyal partner on this trip.

57.
BUMP IN THE ROAD

After two months in Miami, I was ready to move on. I was feeling the usual itch, and I wanted to see more before the seemingly inevitable return to Boston. My next stop would be New Orleans. It was a long drive from Miami, and I was exhausted when I arrived in Louisiana. The city was still locked down, and the usual electric energy I had experienced there before, was on hold. I tried to lure some friends over but nobody could make it work. I walked around for hours and joined yoga classes and tours. These were usually bulletproof ways to meet new people, but I wasn't in the mood. I was disappointed and coming off my Miami high, missing old and new friends.

After what felt like the longest two weeks, I drove to Texas. Fourteen days was too short of a stop to take yet another eight-hour drive. I realized traveling slowly was my preferred way of being a digital nomad, and I felt rushed and exhausted arriving in Austin. Over the past couple of months, I had found a tribe of remote workers and had moderated conversations on all aspects of travel on a social audio app called Clubhouse. Some of the girls had warned me about the risk of burnout, and I was definitely on the verge. The Airbnb was fine, but it didn't give me a warm and fuzzy feeling. By this point, I had been on the road for six months, and my energy level was low. I wondered if this would be the end and If I should go back to Boston and stay with friends. Ava kept saying I didn't have to do this and I could fly back even if it was only for a couple of days. I had set out to cross the country, but I was only doing it for myself. If it didn't feel good, I could turn around or take a break. I decided to give Austin a couple of days and see what my gut told me.

I had started this trip because I knew Boston was not my home and maybe there was a town out there where my heart would give me a sign I had to stay. Was the feeling of being home an actual place or could I cultivate that feeling while I was living a gypsy? Next to my morning practice, I arranged crystals on the nightstand, and pulled some oracle cards every couple of days. These rituals were my attempt to create some grounding while I was floating like a leaf in the wind.

58.
LONE STAR STATE

I downloaded and deleted the dating apps as usual while I was on the road. On my profile, I stated clearly that I was only in a city for a short time, so there were no surprises for anyone involved. What was I even looking for on dating apps? I was on the road, and I hadn't felt the urge to settle anywhere. I figured more travelers were looking to meet new people while on the road or locals wanted to hear about adventures of others. I was looking for company rather than romance. Deep down, I wanted a committed and loving relationship, but I hadn't come across a man with whom I wanted to take the plunge. I also couldn't reconcile that deep need of connecting with my current lifestyle. The first night I was checking out the offer in Austin and one man asked me out for dinner after a short exchange of pleasantries. I preferred this scenario because even though I wasn't looking for a fling, I wasn't looking for a penpal, either.

That very same evening, I walked three blocks from my apartment to the restaurant where I was going to meet this man. He was a couple of years younger than me, a pattern that had emerged since I moved to the States. I had done my best to dress up, I was wearing a nice dress with leopard print, a light denim kimono and new leather sandals I bought that day when I realized I only had sneakers and slides with me on my trip. I put on make-up, and I felt very self-conscious while I walked to the restaurant. Arjun arrived a couple of minutes late. He was wearing jeans and a crisp white shirt. He had a beard and black hair almost touching his shoulders, and he looked like a tall, skinny Indian prince. He was in a rush because he had been waiting for his best friend to watch his eight-week-old puppy. I hadn't come from a family of dog lovers but my best friend Charlie was the biggest dog fan I had ever met. There could be ten strollers with babies passing by and she wouldn't he wouldn't look up, but one puppy, and she would need to pet them, play with them and feed them treats for the next ten minutes. It rubbed off on me, so this man being a dog dad was a plus.

We started the evening with cocktails, and he ordered some appetizers. He was an engineer and worked at a big consulting firm, so I knew he worked extremely long hours. Before he started his job, he had been traveling a lot and stayed at an ashram studying meditation. There were the usual questions about family and career, but we quickly went below the surface as my need for meaningful conversations had only grown stronger the more I traveled and met new people. After our cocktail, he ordered a bottle of champagne. Intoxicated with our good conversation, I agreed to it. It tipped me over the edge of where I wanted to be on a first date. I wanted to stay in control of the situation and make sure nothing happened that I would regret in the morning. We walked out after we finished the bottle and dessert, and since he lived right around the corner, he asked me to come up and meet his puppy. I conceded after seeing some pictures and videos, and when we entered his best friend's apartment, a cute little furball walked up to me and his daddy's plan worked.

I stayed over that night. In the morning, the puppy nestled himself next to me. There was the usual feeling of panic and guilt, not having taken things slow as I specifically urged myself to do, but I would only be in Austin for another couple of weeks. *Maybe this was not the time to take it slow,* my mind tried to convince me. The insecurity and darkness were looming, and the proverbial and literal hangover didn't help. I was on the phone for an hour with my best friend, she knew the drill and was able to calm me down. She asked me what I wanted. I said I would love to spend the rest of my day with him. I gathered up the courage and communicated my wish. He simply replied: "When do you want me to pick you up?"

We spent the day together, talking, taking the puppy out, watching movies, kissing, and making love. He asked me why I wasn't in a relationship, and for the first time I could communicate that when I had been in relationships a lot of fear came up and I couldn't easily relax and be myself. I explained that it might have to do with me losing a twin in the womb, a fact I could never absolutely know if it was true, but every cell in my body was confirming it was. I thought I had been trying to recreate the symbiosis I had experienced with my twin, but that it was too much for a partner, and I would never be able to find that outside of myself. He replied with so much understanding and empathy. He shared his story and similar patterns that he had been keeping alive. I had never had this type of conversation on a Sunday afternoon, and I had never had this type of conversation with a love interest. He walked me home that evening and kissed me goodnight.

That week the darkness came back. I regretted having gone so fast and sharing so much. I should have known better by now. I was afraid that I had ruined everything, and he would be gone. But something was different, the dark hole was not bottomless; it had edges. I could communicate with both Gabrielle and Alexa and tell them how I felt. Before, I could never reach out. He texted me once during the week, but I couldn't tell him how I felt over text, I knew how crazy his schedule was. By Friday, I was pissed, and I had Isabelle coming to see me that weekend, so I wasn't going to give it much more thought. I had missed some of his calls and messages, and I replied with short sentences. I had convinced myself that he wasn't interested anymore, or and I armored myself with the belief that he was not doing his best, so I wouldn't reward him with my presence.

The final week I was in the city, I had to get the sunglasses that I had left at his apartment, and he asked to take me out one more time before I left. I hesitantly agreed. I had feelings for him but was already completely convinced this didn't mean anything to him. When he picked me up with his motorcycle, I was not so secretly happy to see him. When we were sitting at a food truck surrounded with little trays of food from all around the world, he asked me: "So, what happened? We had such a good time, and then you were gone." I was speechless. After he didn't hear from me, he went to my LinkedIn profile to see what job I was doing, so he could understand how busy my week must have been. I explained how I thought he wasn't interested since he didn't text me much that week. He started repeating all the loving things he said to me the week before. I said I thought that he'd changed his mind. We stared at each other with our jaws dropped. We both thought the other wasn't interested. My fear had taken over, and I had projected it onto the situation. As a result, I could no longer see reality. And I was leaving the next day. I was the boss of my itinerary and after he asked to stay another week, I agreed.

The time we spent was wonderful. All the strict rules I usually had to abide by were on hold. The inner critic didn't win this time, and my inner child was happy to be with him. During the day, we worked, and in the evening, we watched comedy specials or action hero movies. We hung out with his friends, who were wonderful, intelligent, funny people. I felt cherished and mentally stimulated, something that had been missing in my relationships in the past. He hinted at a shared future, but I didn't feel like the time was right for us. He was set on staying in Austin since that's where he had his best friends and his dog, but I couldn't see myself settling there. I was still not done traveling and knew I inevitably had to move back to Boston at some point when remote working came to an end. After Oscar, I swore never to do long distance again, but wasn't that the only option while I was on the road? I told him that it didn't feel like I could make a commitment because I had no idea what the future would hold. He was also working so much and not really enjoying it and that was something I was starting to wonder about myself. Was it ever going to end? The calendar was relentless, and it had started to feel machine-like. I had been digging for my purpose and I had a deep yearning to deeply support women. I knew that something would happen, so I could focus on my passion instead of creating more products women didn't need.

I left Austin eight days after I said I would, I wasn't in a relationship, but I had found someone I shared a wonderful moment with and felt love for. And I still chose to leave. There was no bending over backward to be with someone or changing my entire life and persona to make them stay. I was continuing my journey, and that was huge.

59.
A FIFTEEN MINUTE CALL

I finally headed in the direction of Phoenix, Arizona. I was exhausted and not up for a seven hour drive, but I had the week after off to do a tour of the national parks in the area with Ella and my friends. I finished all the work, answered all the emails and finally turned on my out-of-office. We had impressed ourselves planning the eight day trip to a tee, including spreadsheets by day with addresses, dates, timing, and routes. All we had to do was go with the flow. It was the end of April, and the weather was perfect for hiking. Connecting with nature was exactly what I needed on this trip. Eight days without staring at a screen sounded like paradise.

All 4 national parks had such a different sentiment, which made us feel like we covered a lot of ground. Our last stop was Palm Springs. After all the hiking boots, thermal underwear, and hats, we were ready for bathing suits and cocktails by the pool of the Ace Hotel. For forty-eight hours, all we did was relax, eat, get massages and order drinks from the bar. On Sunday, the gang left early, and I had the entire day to rest and get ready for the work week. I had felt a strong urge to stay in Palm Springs for a couple of extra days. I didn't know why but every other hotel looked horrible and bleak compared to the one I was in, so I followed my gut and allowed myself the splurge.

At work, there had been rumblings of a reorganization since the mother company already had gone through an extensive restructuring the year before, and we knew it was coming. On Monday, we got an email from the CEO announcing that in the next two weeks the moment of truth would finally be here. He stated that people would be let go and urged everyone to be respectful and empathetic to other employees' situations. I had been through many of these reorgs in this company and the one I worked for previously. I knew it wasn't personal, but I also didn't think I would be a part of it. I had been with the company for seven years. They moved me twice for my job, so they had already invested a lot in my career. I had never worked as hard as I had the past year, and in December, the company started my green card application.

That day, every-one on my team had received an invite to a fifteen-minute conversation with the VP– except for me. That was odd. I waited all day, but it didn't come. I started making a list of questions I wanted to ask if I was let go. I woke up at 5:00 a.m. in California since I worked on East Coast time. I checked my email, and my appointment was scheduled at 10:30 a.m. and HR was involved, so that couldn't be good. I called my mentors to ask for advice, but that was all I could do. At point, I could only wait for what was to come. I walked around the hotel, got a coffee and a ginger shot, and asked if I could have an office to have my meeting in, but they didn't have any.

The meeting started. The VP was direct and to the point. He said that due to the shifting of the org chart, my job no longer existed. There were some other words, but I barely heard them. For the first time in eight months, the wifi was spotty. They had to ask me to state that I understood the message of the conversation. I held on to the list of questions for dear life even when my vision became blurry from tears. I knew that this could happen, but it was still unreal to go through this again. The only thing I added was that the brand had been an important part of my life and I had given it my all. All the VP could do was nod in agreement since he probably legally couldn't say much else.

And that was it. Life as I knew it was over. Without a job, the country I was exploring was no longer my home-base. The chapter was closed, but somewhere, I felt that the change I had been secretly asking for had finally arrived.

I didn't know what to do, and after making some phone calls, I went down to the lobby and sat by the pool. I ordered a glass of sparkling wine and decided to go for a swim. When I was in the water, I could feel my body relaxing. The question, "When is this going to end?" had been answered. It was over. The career I had frantically pursued and the impasse I found myself in, had dissolved and resolved. While I was sipping my drink by the pool, I knew the future was as bright as the Californian sky, and I was going to be okay.

EPILOGUE

While writing this book, I tried to define my journey as a single woman for months. How much progress had I made? How much have I changed in the past decade? I would dig and dissect for hours, I asked all my close friends and made loads of before and after lists. Could I even call it a journey? And if so, what was the beginning and what was the end?

Over the past couple of years, my intuition and consciousness have grown stronger and started taking the lead. Logic wasn't as dictatorial anymore, and I included my entire body in any decision-making process. The ego wasn't as everpresent, and neither was I trying to prove to everyone that *I could do it*. These changes made way for the question *"What do I want to do?"* That seemed to be the hardest question of all and easily forgotten. Today, I no longer numb myself with alcohol, cigarettes, work or fake love, but instead I look for ways to nourish myself with healing foods, beverages, and practices. I am supportive instead of choosing punishment. I have come to know nature. I pick heart over hard. I have learned how to be by myself, and now, I crave that alone time. When I am by myself, my thoughts are clear and there is no noise. I know what my purpose is. I am here to support women, and that's all I want to do.

The final step is to allow myself to be creative and go into that soft whirling wave of malleable energy without knowing where I will end up.

But the biggest change is that, whether or not I am a new and improved version of myself doesn't matter. I am not this person 100% of the time and that's totally fine, I don't have to be completely evolved every moment of every day. That's just me doing my best again, and it's so freaking rigid. I am applying more kindness to every situation and that's the real change. I am taking the biggest small steps possible and with every little step, I am still evolving. I don't have to do my best to earn anything. Simply being here, I am worthy.

My journey started with looking for a man, and it brought me to myself. The journey doesn't end with me finding a partner, but me feeling like I am worthy of one, even though I don't need him to be whole. Nobody has to make me happy but me. Who am I deep down? How can I authentically lead my life? Those are the questions I remind myself of every single day. And nobody is worth leaving me for.

ACKNOWLEDGEMENTS

Thanks to my parents, brother, sister and my entire family for always being there and loving me.

Thanks to Jacoba an Ruth, you were there from inception to finish and I will always be grateful to you.

Thanks to Daphnee & Simone, for your dedication to this book, this movement and being the personification of female support.

Thanks to Wimsie, for contributing to the success of this book, being a thought partner and being so invested in this project.

Thanks Katie, Lisa & Daisy, for your opinion and late night corrections. You really got a feel for this.

Thanks to Chris from Jetlaunch and Nancy from Zoowrite for making a non native speaker believe she could do it.

Thanks to the people at Audiotheque, Louise-Marie, Mathijs, Stefan, Katrien and Anneke.

Thanks Candy & Ruth, just for being you.

Thanks to Nelleke, Annelies, Emma & Emilie for being my sisters.

Thanks to Lore, for giving me the final push.

Thanks to my angels Lydia, metje Maria and meme Netje for making everything align.

Thanks to all my friends & family all over the world. I couldn't have done it without you.

Join this community of brave women and share your story
on :camera: **@BARE_NAKED_STORIES**

CONTACT THE AUTHOR
Fien@barenakedstories.com

© 2022, Fien Kestelyn, Maison de la femme Publishing
Westerse Clyttestraat 2, 8970 Reningelst, Belgium

Cover & interior design Wim Esteban De Dobbeleer
Editing/production Jetlaunch.net
www.zoowrite.com

ISBN 978-1-64184-789-6